W9-AJO-766

WORLD ⊕ HISTORY

The Vikings

Don Nardo

LUCENT BOOKS
A part of Gale, Cengage Learning

GALE
CENGAGE Learning™

Detroit • New York • San Francisco • New Haven, Conn • Waterville, Maine • London

LIBRARY OF CONGRESS CATALOGING-IN-PUBLICATION DATA

Nardo, Don, 1947-
 The Vikings / by Don Nardo.
    p. cm. -- (World history)
 Includes bibliographical references and index.
 ISBN 978-1-4205-0316-6 (hardcover)
 1. Vikings--Juvenile literature. 2. Northmen--Juvenile literature. 3. Civilization, Viking--Juvenile literature. I. Title.
 DL66.N37 2010
 948'.022--dc22

                                                          2010010500

Lucent Books
27500 Drake Rd.
Farmington Hills, MI 48331

ISBN-13: 978-1-4205-0316-6
ISBN-10: 1-4205-0316-2

Printed in the United States of America
1 2 3 4 5 6 7 14 13 12 11 10

Printed by Bang Printing, Brainerd, MN, 1st Ptg., 09/2010

Contents

Foreword

Each year, on the first day of school, nearly every history teacher faces the task of explaining why his or her students should study history. Many reasons have been given. One is that lessons exist in the past from which contemporary society can benefit and learn. Another is that exploration of the past allows us to see the origins of our customs, ideas, and institutions. Concepts such as democracy, ethnic conflict, or even things as trivial as fashion or mores, have historical roots.

Reasons such as these impress few students, however. If anything, these explanations seem remote and dull to young minds. Yet history is anything but dull. And therein lies what is perhaps the most compelling reason for studying history: History is filled with great stories. The classic themes of literature and drama—love and sacrifice, hatred and revenge, injustice and betrayal, adversity and triumph—fill the pages of history books, feeding the imagination as well as any of the great works of fiction do.

The story of the Children's Crusade, for example, is one of the most tragic in history. In 1212 Crusader fever hit Europe. A call went out from the pope that all good Christians should journey to Jerusalem to drive out the hated Muslims and return the city to Christian control. Heeding the call, thousands of children made the journey. Parents bravely allowed many children to go, and entire communities were inspired by the faith of these small Crusaders. Unfortunately, many boarded ships that were captained by slave traders, who enthusiastically sold the children into slavery as soon as they arrived at their destination. Thousands died from disease, exposure, and starvation on the long march across Europe to the Mediterranean Sea. Others perished at sea.

Another story, from a modern and more familiar place, offers a soul-wrenching view of personal humiliation but also the ability to rise above it. Hatsuye Egami was one of 110,000 Japanese Americans sent to internment camps during World War II. "Since yesterday we Japanese have ceased to be human beings," he wrote in his diary. "We are numbers. We are no longer Egamis, but the number 23324. A tag with that number is on every trunk, suitcase and bag. Tags, also, on our breasts." Despite such dehumanizing treatment, most internees worked hard to control their bitterness. They created workable communities inside the camps and demonstrated again and again their loyalty as Americans.

These are but two of the many stories from history that can be found in the pages of the Lucent Books World History series. All World History titles rely on sound research and verifiable evidence, and all give students a clear sense of time, place, and chronology through maps and timelines as well as text.

All titles include a wide range of authoritative perspectives that demonstrate the complexity of historical interpretation and sharpen the reader's critical thinking skills. Formally documented quotations and annotated bibliographies enable students to locate and evaluate sources, often instantaneously via the Internet, and serve as valuable tools for further research and debate.

Finally, Lucent's World History titles present rousing good stories, featuring vivid primary source quotations drawn from unique, sometimes obscure sources such as diaries, public records, and contemporary chronicles. In this way, the voices of participants and witnesses as well as important biographers and historians bring the study of history to life. As we are caught up in the lives of others, we are reminded that we too are characters in the ongoing human saga, and we are better prepared for our own roles.

Important Dates at the

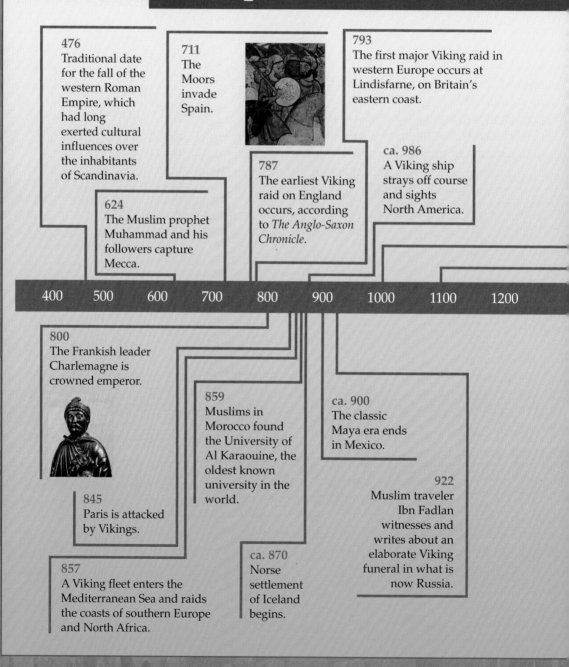

476
Traditional date for the fall of the western Roman Empire, which had long exerted cultural influences over the inhabitants of Scandinavia.

711
The Moors invade Spain.

793
The first major Viking raid in western Europe occurs at Lindisfarne, on Britain's eastern coast.

624
The Muslim prophet Muhammad and his followers capture Mecca.

787
The earliest Viking raid on England occurs, according to *The Anglo-Saxon Chronicle*.

ca. 986
A Viking ship strays off course and sights North America.

400   500   600   700   800   900   1000   1100   1200

800
The Frankish leader Charlemagne is crowned emperor.

859
Muslims in Morocco found the University of Al Karaouine, the oldest known university in the world.

ca. 900
The classic Maya era ends in Mexico.

845
Paris is attacked by Vikings.

922
Muslim traveler Ibn Fadlan witnesses and writes about an elaborate Viking funeral in what is now Russia.

857
A Viking fleet enters the Mediterranean Sea and raids the coasts of southern Europe and North Africa.

ca. 870
Norse settlement of Iceland begins.

Time of the Vikings

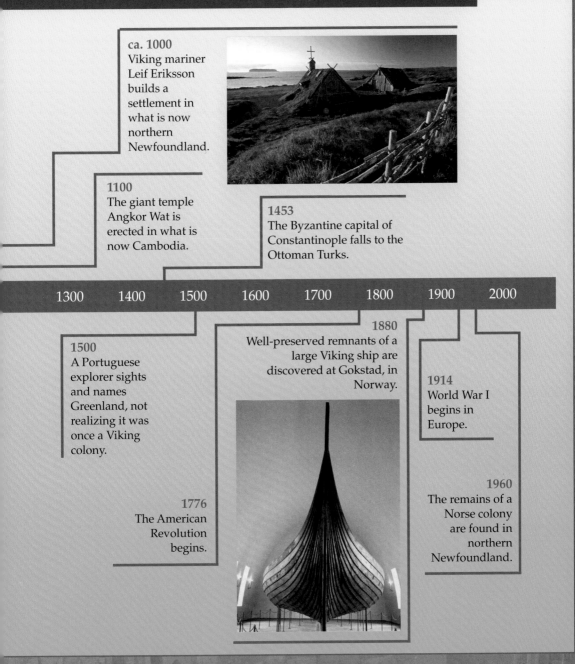

ca. 1000
Viking mariner Leif Eriksson builds a settlement in what is now northern Newfoundland.

1100
The giant temple Angkor Wat is erected in what is now Cambodia.

1453
The Byzantine capital of Constantinople falls to the Ottoman Turks.

1300   1400   1500   1600   1700   1800   1900   2000

1500
A Portuguese explorer sights and names Greenland, not realizing it was once a Viking colony.

1880
Well-preserved remnants of a large Viking ship are discovered at Gokstad, in Norway.

1914
World War I begins in Europe.

1776
The American Revolution begins.

1960
The remains of a Norse colony are found in northern Newfoundland.

Surviving Evidence for the Vikings

For the people of Europe in the early medieval era, the story of the Vikings was one of unexpected and naked violence, of the triumph of the strong and ruthless, and of the suffering of the weak and innocent. The prelude to this epic tale of woe was rooted in late ancient times. In the final century of the Roman Empire, spanning the 400s A.D., tribal peoples from across northern Europe began migrating. Searching for new lands, economic opportunities, and often simply booty, they steadily invaded, overran, and absorbed the empire's outlying provinces. As a result, in the year 476 that realm officially ceased to exist.

This was only the beginning of the bedlam, disorder, and instability Europe was destined to suffer. "With the collapse of the Roman Empire," British Museum scholar David M. Wilson remarks, "the movements [of peoples] became almost frenetic. Huns, Goths, Vandals, wave upon wave of tribes, moved across Europe, giving momentum to the peoples of the continent."[1]

In time, these huge folk migrations finally ran their course. By the late 700s A.D. large sections of Europe had finally settled down and become relatively stable. The era of peace proved to be tragically short-lived, however. In the late eighth century a new source of mayhem and insecurity appeared, this one centered in Scandinavia, the region now encompassed by Denmark, Sweden, and Norway. Marauding bands of raiders from those lands descended on Europe. They had various names, including Norse, Norsemen, and Northmen. But they were (and still are) better known as the Vikings.

The Viking raiders typically struck quickly and with overwhelming force. They stole, pillaged, and frequently murdered with abandon. These raiders struck fear into the hearts of people in many

A band of Viking raiders loots a European village, spreading destruction and fear.

lands, stretching from England and Ireland in the west, across Europe, to what are now Russia and Iran in the east. In the two and a half centuries that followed—the so-called Viking Age—people of diverse cultures and languages had reason to express sentiments like those of an anonymous medieval Irish chronicler. Even if there were a hundred "loud, unceasing voices from each tongue," he said,

they could not recount or narrate . . . what all the Irish suffered in common, both men and women, laity and clergy, old and young, noble and ignoble, of hardships and of injuring and of oppression, in every house, from those valiant, wrathful, purely pagan people [the Vikings] because of the greatness of their achievements and of their deeds, their bravery, and their . . . strength, and their venom, and their ferocity.[2]

The Written Sources

Eventually, the Vikings faded from view as they were absorbed into the populations of dozens of medieval kingdoms. But their impact, both during and after the Viking Age, cannot be overstated. Through raiding, conquest, trade, colonization, and intermarriage, they changed forever the face of Europe and several lands bordering it. Indeed, much of today's world is the result of the deeds and influence of the Vikings a thousand years ago.

Because the Vikings' impact was so large and consequential, historians and other modern experts naturally would like to know as much about them as possible. That information comes from a wide array of sources, which fall into two general categories. The first consists of surviving medieval writings of various types. A few of these are histories or at least earnest attempts to record important events on a regular basis.

The chief example is *The Anglo-Saxon Chronicle*, which English scribes began compiling circa A.D. 890 at the request of their ruler Alfred the Great. Separate entries were made for years both before and after that date. Most of these entries are short and lack detail, but they are helpful in establishing the major annual events affecting England and its vicinity. The first mention of the Vikings appears in the entry for the year 787. The chroniclers called them Northmen, Danes, and/or heathens (non-Christians), as the term *Viking* had not yet been coined. In that year, the *Chronicle* says, "came first three ships of the Northmen from the land of robbers. The [local sheriff] then rode [to the shore to meet them] . . . ; for he knew not what they were; and there was he slain. These were the first ships of the Danish men that sought [to rob and invade] the land of the English nation."[3] Later entries recorded other incursions (invasions) by the Scandinavian raiders, including one for the year 794, which also mentions some Viking ships capsizing in a storm:

In the meantime, the heathen armies spread devastation among the Northumbrians [residents of

This page of The Anglo-Saxon Chronicle, *dating from the mid-eleventh century, mentions a battle fought between the Vikings and English.*

northeastern England] and plundered the monastery of King Everth at the mouth of the Wear. There, however, some of their leaders were slain; and some of their ships also were shattered to pieces by the violence of the weather [and] many of the crew were drowned.[4]

Some other surviving written sources from that period take the form of personal memoirs or travelogues. The storytellers and writers of these tracts often provided valuable information about the everyday lives, habits, and exploits of specific Vikings or of Norsemen in general. One of those storytellers was himself Norse—Ohthere (or Ottar), who dwelled in Norway in the late 800s. In his account he talks about the difficulties of farming in the far north and describes how he hunted walruses for their precious tusks, which he traded, along with other items, in Scandinavian markets. He also tells about a side trip he took to explore the little-known lands lying north of Norway, near the frozen Arctic.

Of particular interest among these personal accounts is that of an early tenth-century Muslim traveler named Ibn Fadlan. Describing the Vikings who had settled in what is now Russia, he recorded for posterity a number of Norse customs, including their rather insensitive treatment of sick people:

When one of them falls ill, they erect a tent away from them and cast him into it, giving him some bread and water. They do not come near him or speak to him, indeed they have no contact with him for the duration of his illness, especially if he is socially inferior or is a slave. If he recovers and gets back to his feet, he rejoins them. If he dies, they bury him, though if he was a slave they leave him there as food for the dogs and the birds.[5]

The Sagas

Among the more important written sources about the Vikings are the Icelandic sagas, a collection of stories written by various authors in Norse-inhabited Iceland not long after the close of the Viking Age. Consisting of prose with sections of poems sometimes embedded in the text, they deal with Scandinavian and German heroes, most of them Vikings. Many of the sagas have mythological and/or highly romanticized elements. Yet many others feature long sections based on real people and incidents, including battles, political alliances, marriages, and voyages of exploration. "These stories paint a vivid picture of the Vikings," writes archaeologist Richard Hall, "not only in Iceland, but across a vast territorial sweep from [eastern North America] to Byzantium [on the Black Sea's southern shore]. Classic accounts of the deeds of heroes, or epic tales of love, passion, greed, and honor, they are a vital part of the Iceland [and Viking] legacy."[6]

That these stories were a liberal mix of real events and some exaggerations and fabrications was freely admitted by the greatest of the Icelandic storytellers—

Exploring the Far North

Norwegian Viking trader Ohthere recited an account of some of his travels, including a brief voyage to the region lying north of his homeland. Referring to himself and companions in the third person, he said:

He was determined to find out . . . how far this country extended northward, or whether any one lived to the north of the waste. With this intent he proceeded northward along the coast, leaving all the way the wasteland on the starboard [the vessel's right side], and the wide sea on the backboard [the vessel's left side], for three days. He was then as far north as the whale-hunters ever go. He then continued his voyage, steering yet northward, as far as he could sail within three other days. . . . He sailed thence along the coast southward, as far as he could in five days. There lay then a great river a long way up in the land, in to the mouth of which they entered. . . . All the land to his right during his whole voyage, was uncultivated and without inhabitants, except a few fishermen, fowlers, and hunters, all of whom were Finlanders; and he had nothing but the wide sea on his left all the way.

Amanda Graham, "The Voyage of Ohthere from King Alfred's *Orosius*," Yukon College, 2001. http://ycdl4 .yukoncollege.yk.ca/~agraham//nost202/ottar.htm.

Snorri Sturluson. A thirteenth-century historian and poet, he composed the *Heimskringla*, a collection of sagas about the kings of Norway who reigned from about A.D. 850 to 1177. In his preface Snorri writes:

In this book I have had old stories written down, as I have heard them told by intelligent people, concerning chiefs who have held dominion in the northern countries, and who spoke the Danish tongue [as well as Norwegian]; and also concerning some of their family branches, according to what has been told me. Some of this is found in ancient family registers, in which the pedigrees of kings and other personages of high birth are reckoned up, and part is written down after old songs and ballads which our forefathers had for their amusement. Now, although we cannot just say what truth there may be in these, yet we have the certainty that old and wise men held them to be true.[7]

Perhaps the most talked-about Viking sagas in the past few decades have been

Erik the Red's Saga and the *Greenlanders' Saga*, which describe Viking voyages from colonies in Greenland to nearby North America. At one time these were thought to have dealt mostly with legendary events and deeds. Beginning in the 1960s, exciting physical evidence confirming these voyages was discovered in Newfoundland. Today these stories, though not taken completely at face value by experts, are viewed as quasi-historical documents.

The Evidence from the Dirt

The physical evidence from Newfoundland—consisting of vestiges of the Viking colony of Leifsbudir (now called L'Anse aux Meadows)—is a prime example of the second major category of surviving information about the Vikings. It consists of archaeological remains, or artifacts—in a sense the evidence taken from the dirt. Included are the remnants of houses, ships, tools, swords and other weapons, grooming items, clothing, coins, wood carvings and other art, and actual human remains.

A great deal of Viking archaeological evidence was uncovered in the twentieth century. Besides that at L'Anse aux Meadows, one of the most famous excavations (archaeological digs) was of the town of Hedeby, on the southern edge of Jutland (the large peninsula making up most of modern Denmark). A trading center that flourished from the eighth through the eleventh centuries, Hedeby was the largest Norse town during the Viking Age, with perhaps a thousand or more residents.

Modern excavations of that settlement took place from 1900 to 1915, 1930 to 1939, and 1959 to the present. Impressively, these have yielded more than 340,000 artifacts, including houses, clothing, pottery and other craft goods, iron tools, coins, ships from the harbor, and skeletons and grave goods from more than 350 human burials. So many well-preserved objects have been found that in 2005, experts felt confident in beginning on-site construction of several exact copies of the town's original houses.

Another important archaeological site where Viking history and culture have come to life is in northeastern England. In the early 800s that region was occupied by the small English kingdom of Northumbria. In 867 a large group of Vikings captured its biggest town, Eoforwic, and changed its name to Jorvik (pronounced yor'-wik). The town flourished as a Norse stronghold for two more centuries. In the ages that followed, Jorvik became York, one of England's leading cities. By the twentieth century the old Viking ruins were buried beneath the modern streets. But in 1976 excavations began in a section of town called Coppergate. Since that time the digs have unearthed a huge array of artifacts, among them houses, barrels, jars, combs, jewelry, and seeds and other surviving remnants of the foodstuffs consumed by the Viking inhabitants. "Together with more durable relics of stone, metal, bone and pottery," one modern observer points out,

These sod houses at L'Anse aux Meadows, in Newfoundland, are replicas of the ones the Vikings erected there more than a thousand years ago.

these discoveries have made it possible for the Jorvik Center in Coppergate to create a detailed picture of life in early medieval times. The Center's pictorial reconstructions [of daily life] are all based on sound archaeological evidence, right down to the lichen the Vikings used to dye cloth and the precise weave of the clothes and socks they wore. One of the most complete and rare finds at Jorvik was a 10th century sock, knitted from wool on a single needle. . . . In addition, experts have recreated the facial appearance of the town's inhabitants based upon skulls retrieved from the cemetery near the site where the Viking Age cathedral may have stood.[8]

As excavations continue at these and other sites across Scandinavia, England, and mainland Europe, the Viking Age and its inhabitants are increasingly coming to light and life. More and more, Hall says, the discovery of new evidence "has brought virtually all aspects of Viking life within the archaeologists' view." Coupled with ongoing studies of the written records, this inflow of new knowledge allows historians "to unlock the world of the Vikings,"[9] whose exploits profoundly shaped late medieval European civilization.

Chapter One

Viking Origins and Early Raids

At some unknown date in the ninth century, an Irish monk was undergoing the then mundane duty of copying a Christian manuscript. Suddenly he felt motivated to scribble some words in the margin of the page he was working on. These words, in the form of a rhyming couplet, survived the centuries and read: "There's a wicked wind tonight, wild upheaval in the sea. No fear now that the Viking hordes will terrify me."[10]

This message by a fearful churchman acknowledged a painful reality of that time and place. Only in inclement weather, when the open sea was too dangerous for sailors, were the coasts of Ireland and nearby lands safe from the Viking menace. Indeed, the monk must have been particularly afraid because for a long time these scary raiders paid special attention to Christian churches and monasteries. This was partly because these places were known to possess gold

and silver crosses, cups, and other objects, along with expensive gifts donated by worshippers of all walks of life.

So it was at St. Cuthbert's in June 793. One of the holiest and richest shrines in the British Isles, this church on the tiny island of Lindisfarne, off Britain's eastern coast, became the unlucky target of the first major Viking raid in Christian Europe. After the attackers had looted the island's buildings and made their escape, a shocked Christian scholar named Alcuin, who lived in the nearby mainland town of Eoforwic (York), writes:

Never before has such terror appeared in Britain, as we have now suffered from a pagan [non-Christian] race. Nor was it thought possible that such an inroad from the sea could be made. Behold the Church of St. Cuthbert, spattered with the blood of the priests of God, despoiled of all its ornaments. A place more venerable

This aerial view shows the ruins of St, Cuthbert's, on the island of Lindisfarne, the first major Christian shrine despoiled by Viking raiders in the eighth century.

[dignified and respected] than any other in Britain has fallen prey to pagans.[11]

The charge that these raiders were pagans at first seemed to derive from the fact that they wantonly attacked churches. The fact is that in those days European Christians of various stripes periodically conducted similar pirate raids; however, as a rule they refrained from assaulting churches and monasteries, hence the particular disdain for the newly arrived pagan foreigners.

Out of the Northern Mists

The victims of Lindisfarne and other initial targets of the raids had two burning questions. First, who were these seemingly godless foreigners; and second, where had they come from? It did not take long to identify them as Scandinavians, hailing from the largely barren and cold lands in Europe's northernmost reaches.

Why, then, did they come to be called Vikings instead of Scandinavians, or perhaps Norwegians or Swedes? Searching for the derivation of the term *Viking*, modern scholars found an old Norse word (that is, a word in Old Norse, the Germanic language spoken in Scandinavia in those days)—*vikingr*. It appears to have been a noun that described men who went *"i viking,"* or became involved in raiding or piracy. "In this sense," University of Lancaster scholar John Haywood explains,

> most Viking-age Scandinavians were not Vikings at all, but peaceful farmers and craftsmen who stayed quietly at home all their lives. For many others, being a Viking was just an occupation they resorted to for long enough to raise the money to buy, or otherwise acquire, a farm and settle down. [Nevertheless] the wider use of "Viking" is too well established to insist on using the word only in the narrow meaning of "pirate."[12]

Saxo Describes Jutland

In his History of the Danes, *twelfth-century Danish historian Saxo Grammaticus said the following about the geography of Jutland, Denmark's main peninsula:*

Denmark is cut in pieces by the intervening waves of ocean, and has but few portions of firm and continuous territory; these being divided by the mass of waters that break them up, in ways varying with the different angle of the bend of the sea. Of all these, Jutland, being the largest and first settled, holds the chief place in the Danish kingdom. It both lies foremost and stretches furthest, reaching to the frontiers of Teutonland [Germany], from contact with which it is severed by the bed of the river Eyder. Northwards it swells somewhat in breadth, and runs out to the shore of the Noric Channel (Skagerrak). In this part is to be found the fjord called Liim, which is so full of fish that it seems to yield the natives as much food as the whole soil.

Saxo Grammaticus, *History of the Danes*, Northvegr Foundation. www.northvegr.org/lore/saxo/000_14.php.

Whatever later ages came to call the residents of medieval Scandinavia, including those who went out raiding, scholars would also like to know how they rose to such prominence and military and economic success. But extremely little is known about them before they suddenly burst out of Europe's northern mists in the late eighth and early ninth centuries. One certainty is that once they did emerge from the northern wilds, the region of extreme northwestern Europe became one of their main stomping grounds. It included Britain, Ireland, and the islands lying north of them, including the Shetlands and Iceland, all lying directly west of Scandinavia.

The first known European to explore that larger region was the late-fourth-

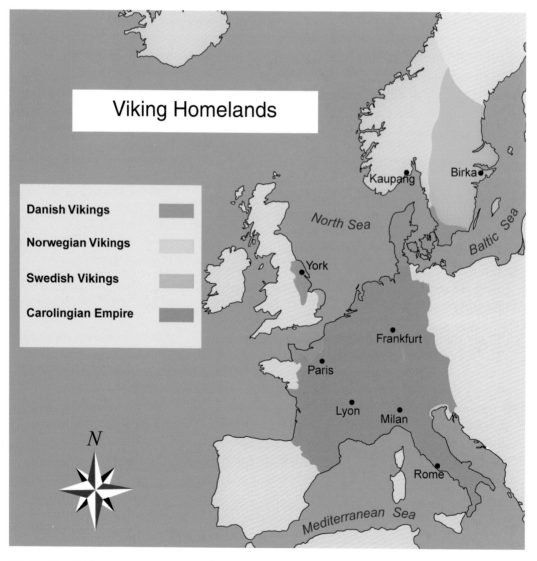

Viking Homelands

Danish Vikings

Norwegian Vikings

Swedish Vikings

Carolingian Empire

Kaupang

Birka

North Sea

Baltic Sea

York

Frankfurt

Paris

Lyon

Milan

Rome

Mediterranean Sea

N

century B.C. Greek sea captain Pytheas. After crossing what is now the English Channel, he headed slowly northward between Britain and Ireland and rounded Scotland. Then he investigated the Orkney and Shetland islands lying north of the British Isles. He may have later reached Thule, or Iceland, and some experts think he managed to cross the Arctic Circle before huge blocks of ice forced him to turn back. Pytheas's book about his travels has not survived. But four centuries later, in the first century A.D., famous Roman naturalist Pliny the Elder read it. He writes:

> The parts of the Earth that lie at the poles have continuous daylight for six months at a time and continuous night for six months when the sun has withdrawn in the opposite direction towards midwinter. Pytheas of Massalia writes that this happens in the island of Thule, six days [by boat] north of Britain.[13]

By Pliny's day, a few Roman traders had ventured into Scandinavia itself. And his contemporary, Roman historian Tacitus, briefly mentions that area's residents in one of his own treatises. Most memorably, he singles out the Swedes, whom he calls the Suiones. He pays particular attention to their ships, which were clearly the forerunners of Viking vessels, the main difference being that the earlier versions had no sails:

> They [the Suiones] are powerful, not only in arms and men but also in

fleets. The shape of their ships differs from the normal in having a prow at each end, so that they are always facing the right way to put into shore. They do not propel them with sails, nor do they fasten a row of oars to the sides. The rowlocks are movable [and] can be reversed, as circumstances require, for rowing in either direction.[14]

Roman Cultural Influences

Modern archaeologists have shown that these early Swedes, like other Scandinavians of the period, were mostly farmers who raised livestock and/or grew crops using rudimentary plows and other tools. They also supplemented their diets by hunting and fishing. Culturally speaking, they were backward compared to the contemporary Mediterranean civilizations of Greece and Rome. For that reason, the highly cultured Greeks and Romans lumped them together with other Germanic tribal groups whom they collectively referred to, unfavorably, as "barbarians."

One major mark against the early Scandinavians in Greco-Roman eyes was that, at the time, those northern European folk had no towns or cities. Rome had a million residents, and many other towns in its realm had populations in the tens or hundreds of thousands. But all Scandinavians then dwelled either on their remote rural farms or in very small villages of no more than a couple hundred people. Other reasons the early Scandinavians appeared primitive to the Roman world were that they as yet had no written laws, no literature, and no formal schools.

While the Romans looked down on the residents of Scandinavia, the reverse was not the case, in part *because* of Rome's more advanced culture. Some of the artistic styles of the early Scandinavians were original to their own lands. However, they could not help but be culturally influenced by the strongest, most widespread, and most envied culture of that era—that of Rome. In the first few centuries A.D., the Roman Empire stretched across all of southern Europe and also included Britain, North Africa (including Egypt), and large sections of the Middle East. In many ways Rome was the envy of and cultural model for the known world. For that reason, the tribal societies of what would later become Denmark, Norway, and Sweden often borrowed artistic, clothing, and jewelry styles from the Romans. (Often this happened indirectly, through contact with the Germanic tribes who dwelled in the lands sandwiched between Scandinavia and Roman territory.) According to Wilson:

> The shapes and designs of the armrings, brooches and gold pendants worn by [early Scandinavian] men and women, and the forms of some of the pottery which was used for both cooking and storage, were based to some extent on Roman models. Roman ornamental motifs were incorporated into their own

art. Occasionally they even attempted to reproduce Roman representational art in their own idiom [personal style]. Provincial Roman statues were copied [and] Roman designs formed the basis for the lively art [of early Scandinavia].[15]

A clear example of Rome's artistic influences on early, and ultimately later Scandinavian art is the zoomorphic artistic style embraced by both the Vikings' immediate ancestors and the Vikings themselves. Zoomorphic artistic motifs are built around representations of animals. Over the years, Roman coins, medallions, drinking cups, and other artifacts decorated with animal motifs (and often made of gold) made their way, via trade, into Scandinavia. The locals adopted these artistic ideas, producing their own artistic works in the zoomorphic style. These included medallion-like artifacts called bracteates, along with rings, brooches, belt buckles, sword hilts, drinking cups, ship prows, and other ornamental objects.

Economic Expansion

In the first few centuries A.D., in which Roman civilization was culturally influencing Scandinavia from afar, Rome itself was in a steady state of political decline. During those centuries, as well as in the three centuries that followed the empire's collapse in the late 400s, the Scandinavians were growing more populous, more politically stable, and better off economically. "Although never free from internal trouble," Wilson explains,

This first-century B.C. embossed silver sculpture, showing the Celtic fertility god Cerunnos, was influenced by Roman artistic styles.

"the Scandinavians were building up a self-confident civilization of their own between A.D. 400 and 800." And that civilization "reached its full-blooded maturity with the Viking adventure."[16]

Several factors contributed to this continuing upsurge in the fortunes and capabilities of Scandinavia's early peoples. First, the generally substandard soils of much of their region forced them to turn to shipbuilding and the sea to make a hefty portion of their livings. Their maritime activities included fishing and hunting seal and walrus and, to an even greater degree, trade. Over time, producing and acquiring a wide range of trade items made many Scandinavians better able to support themselves. This led to increasing economic expansion, which in turn stimulated more population growth.

In Denmark, that growth was further fueled by two other factors. One was that the area's soil was rich enough to support a fair amount of crop production, making food more plentiful there than in Norway and Sweden. Also, fishing in the Baltic Sea around Denmark's large island of Zealand was particularly plentiful and financially lucrative. Twelfth-century Danish historian Saxo Grammaticus, who penned a history of his people, writes:

[Facing Jutland] on the east [is] Zealand, which is famed for its remark-

Living with Limited Usable Land

University of York scholar Julian D. Richards supplies this concise description of the rather limited usable lands available to the Vikings of Norway:

Norway took its name from the sheltered sea route down its western coast, the *Norvegur*, or "North Way." The coastline is indented by countless fjords [long, narrow channels, often lined with cliffs]. Measured in a direct line it is 3,000 kilometers [1,860 miles], but its real length is 20,000 kilometers [12,400 miles]. Mountains arise directly from the western coast and the Viking age population was confined to narrow ledges and small plains at the heads of the fjords, where communities developed in relative isolation, each with its own traditions and culture. More than half of the country lies at altitudes above 600 meters [1,968 feet], but there are just a few fertile areas of gentle slopes where population is concentrated. . . . Even today, agricultural land accounts for only 3 percent of the surface area [of Norway].

Julian D. Richards, *The Vikings: A Very Short Introduction*. New York: Oxford University Press, 2005, p. 15.

able richness in the necessaries of life. This latter island, being by far the most delightful of all the provinces of our country, is held to occupy the heart of Denmark, being divided by equal distances from the extreme frontier; on its eastern side the [Baltic] sea breaks through and cuts off the western side of Skaane [Scania, or southern Sweden, then a part of Denmark]; and this sea commonly yields each year an abundant haul to the nets of the fishers. Indeed, the whole sound is apt to be so thronged with fish that any craft which strikes on them is with difficulty got off by hard rowing, and the prize is captured no longer by tackle, but by simple use of the hands.[17]

Emergence of a Predatory Society

Another factor in the growing strength and versatility of Scandinavian civilization was the emergence of more martial, or aggressive and warlike, elements of society. In this the Scandinavians got their cue, in a sense, from what was happening with their distant cousins, the Germanic tribes living in the lands north of the Alps and south of Denmark. Prolonged trade and cultural contact with Rome had steadily enriched the Germans in all manner of goods, from gold to textiles to weapons. In the 300s and 400s small bands of Scandinavians began raiding the Germanic lands to acquire some of this loot.

The Danes and other Scandinavians were also influenced by ongoing German social and political developments, including the formation of warrior bands, each led by a strong chief. The warriors remained loyal to their chief as long as he guided them to exploits that enriched them. According to Haywood:

> Military expeditions to win plunder and tribute [money or valuables paid to acknowledge submission] created a very competitive, predatory society where success in war was the key to power and status. It also led to the concentration of power in fewer and fewer hands and to the merging of tribes, either voluntarily to wage war . . . or because a weaker tribe had been conquered by a stronger. It was probably in this way, for example, that the Danes emerged as the dominant people of southern Scandinavia by the 6th century.[18]

As more Scandinavians copied this model and became increasingly militaristic, they began building large-scale fortifications in their lands. Archaeologists have found evidence for at least fifteen hundred such defenses built between A.D. 400 and 600. They may have been intended not only for local security but also to delineate and defend small local chiefdoms or kingdoms that started to appear toward the end of this period. At least ten of these early political units developed, mostly along the coasts. One was in east-central Sweden, around a site called Gamla Uppsala. Another appeared in Denmark in the

Chiefs of the Scandinavian kingdom centered at Gamla Uppsala were buried beneath these earthen mounds, which today are tourist attractions.

700s, possibly centered at Ribe (Denmark's oldest town), in southwestern Jutland.

Small trading centers were built to facilitate exchanges of goods among these chiefdoms, some of which would, centuries later, become the medieval nations of Denmark, Sweden, and Norway. These centers increasingly became personal power bases for strong, enterprising warrior-chiefs who wanted to get rich and make names for themselves at the same time. Some evidence shows that, in Hall's words, "The ever-growing political power of Scandinavian kings encouraged chieftains to bolster their waning status in the homeland by seeking the large and instant rewards that could be gained in lucrative overseas ventures."[19]

The Viking Menace

Thus, steady increases in population, increased trade, the growth of forceful military cliques, and the rise of small kingdoms all contributed to the development of an economically and militarily stronger and more robust Scandinavian society. It was perhaps inevitable that some sectors of this society would eventually seek to expand their opportunities by venturing beyond their homelands. And their excellent command of ships and seafaring, which had developed over the preceding centuries, made this expansion both possible and enticing.

The overall result was the sudden burst of Viking raids that began at Lindisfarne in 793. These early attacks, lasting from the 790s to about 834, had several factors in common. First, they were relatively small—usually consisting of ten or twelve ships at most. Second, the raiders almost always confined their nefarious activities to the coasts of the lands they plundered, at first consisting mainly of Britain, Ireland, Francia (France), and Frisia (northwestern Germany). Also, the incursions were nearly always brief and of a hit-and-run nature.

A squadron of Viking warships passes by a rugged coastline on its way to raid European settlements.

This approach was designed to frustrate local military forces, which usually had no idea where the attacks would occur and were therefore unable to rush to the rescue in time.

In addition, a large percentage of the targets were churches and monasteries, and not only because these places possessed accumulated wealth. The early Vikings may have been uncultured, but they were often quite canny and clever in political and military matters. A number of modern experts suggest, as one of them puts it, that

> this was a deliberate targeting of the sites which provided the religious and ideological underpinning of west European Christianity. [It was] an attempt, in other words, of a form of psychological warfare, with the aims of undermining the west European belief system and showing that the Christians' god was not omnipotent but vulnerable, and not superior to the gods of Scandinavia.[20]

Finally, most of the early Viking raids occurred in the warmer months, when seafaring was easier and safer, and the ships returned to Scandinavia in the winter. This gave the residents of coastal northeastern Europe a welcome breather from the ongoing and frightening Norse threat. In time, however, such respites became a thing of the past. A new phase of the Viking menace was about to begin, one in which sporadic raiding would be replaced by major attempts at conquest and settlement. Some Vikings were no longer content simply with tiny pieces of the European pie. Much to the horror of the inhabitants of inland areas who thought they were relatively safe, the part-time attackers became full-time invaders.

Chapter Two

Viking Conquests and Expansion

Year after year, Christian churchmen and members of their flocks alike recited the Latin words *A furore Normannorum libra nos, Domine!* which in English means "From the fury of the Northmen deliver us, O Lord!"[21] This or similar anxious phrases echoed across western Europe throughout the initial period of Viking incursions—from the 790s to early 830s.

Hundreds of raids occurred in these years. Among the more infamous were those on the Colmcille monastery on the Scottish island of Iona and the church on Lambey Island, in eastern Ireland, both in 795. These attacks were ruthless and brutal, to be sure. In a later raid on Iona, Viking warriors slaughtered eighty-six monks without mercy on the beach adjoining the monastery. (The nearby waters are still called the Bay of the Martyrs in honor of the fallen churchmen.)

Yet despite such horrors, what seemed a small saving grace for many of the victims was that the vast majority of the assaults were brief. The raiders typically struck, gathered their loot, and then departed, leaving the local survivors to regroup and rebuild. Sometimes the Vikings came back and hit the same target again, as in the case of Iona, which suffered at least four raids in that period (in 795, 802, 806, and 825). Still, the pirates could at least be counted on to return each winter to their homelands, which lay far away to the east.

Ominous Changes in Tactics

This situation soon changed. In the early 830s the Viking raiders started altering their tactics in ominous ways. First, the number of yearly attacks increased markedly. So did the size of the raiding parties, as many Viking fleets grew in size to as many as thirty to thirty-five ships, and in the decades

This modern reconstruction shows the Viking longphort, or fortified coastal base, on the island of Zealand, in medieval Denmark.

that followed a few had as many as a hundred vessels.

Even more disconcerting for the victims, the raiders' ships began sailing far upstream on the larger, navigable rivers, which allowed them to ravage inland areas. In Ireland in 836, for instance, a Viking fleet moved up the Shannon River and sacked the important monastery at Clonmacnoise, in the island's heartland. Similar forays were

launched up the Rhine River in Germany and the Loire and Seine rivers in France.

Next, in the late 830s and early 840s, many Viking raiders ceased returning to Scandinavia each winter. Instead, they built *longphorts*, fortified coastal bases, on the shores of Germany and France and later Ireland and Scotland. Raiding parties spent the winter at such bases, allowing them to get an earlier and easier start in the next raiding season. The tremendous advantage this gave the Vikings can be seen by what happened when such overwintering began in England in 850 or 851. *The Anglo-Saxon Chronicle* recorded that "The heathens now for the first time remained over winter in the Isle of Thanet." Thanet is located near the tip of Kent, in southeastern England, a strategic spot where the raiders were able to take the time to amass a huge force for their coming campaign. According to the *Chronicle*: "The same year came three hundred and fifty ships into the mouth of the Thames [River]; the crew of which went upon land, and stormed Canterbury and London, putting to flight Bertulf [a local king], with his army, and then marched southward over the Thames into Surrey [to conduct more raids]."[22]

Most disquieting of all was when large Viking groups decided to forego ordinary raiding and pursue large-scale conquest and settlement. This happened in many parts of western Europe, most noticeably at first in southeastern England. In 865, *The Anglo-Saxon Chronicle* recorded, the Viking forces wintering at Thanet "made peace with the men of Kent, who promised money." Paying such money, essentially a bribe to guarantee that the intruders would not pillage the countryside, was becoming a common tactic among the Vikings' victims. The English called it "Danegold," a reference to the fact that many of the raiders were Danes. In any case, the Vikings took the money and then double-crossed the "men of Kent." The *Chronicle*

tells how "under the security of peace, and the promise of money, the [Viking] army in the night stole up the country, and overran all Kent eastward."[23] In the years that followed, more and more English and other European lands fell to the invaders.

Modern scholars have frequently debated about why some Vikings resorted to the conquest and settlement of foreign lands. Those scholars generally agree that it was not because the small amount of decent farmland in Scandinavia could no longer support the growing population. Instead, such conquests appear to have been a way for some of the more determined and competing Viking leaders to create their own power bases outside the homelands. As Hall points out, the conquered lands

were arenas where ambitious and successful warriors with only a relatively low social standing in their homeland could escape those constraints, dramatically improve their fortunes, and become their own masters. The careers of some leaders suggest that they were not mere opportunists, but were prepared to assault target after target in dogged pursuit of a territory over which they could exert control.[24]

Targeting the Franks

Whatever their motives may have been, from the early 800s on, the Vikings employed a mix of aggressive tactics against foreign lands, including large-scale raids, the creation of winter bases,

All Five Brothers Dead

In their wide-ranging forays into foreign lands, the Vikings took enormous risks, and sometimes they suffered equally large setbacks. A surviving rune inscription tells about the deaths of five brothers from a single Swedish family:

The good farmer Gulle had five sons. At Fyris fell Asmund, the unfrightened warrior; Assur died out east in Greece [i.e., the Byzantine lands]; Halvdan was in [a] duel slain; Kare died at [Dundee?]; dead is Boe, too.

Quoted in Howard La Fay, *The Vikings.* Washington, DC: National Geographic, 1972, p. 79.

and invasions and attempts to set up small kingdoms, as local circumstances seemed to warrant them. A clear example of this mixed approach can be seen in the way the Vikings targeted the Franks throughout much of the ninth century.

The early medieval Franks were the direct forerunners of the French, Belgians, Dutch, and western Germans. During the Viking Age, large Frankish kingdoms covered much of what are now France, Belgium, the Netherlands, and Germany. Some early Viking raids occurred along the Frankish coasts, from the mouth of the Seine River northward to Frisia, between 799 and 820. Many of the attackers were driven away because Frankish coastal defenses were strong and well organized. But as happened in England, Ireland, and elsewhere, the raids on the Franks sharply increased in intensity in the 830s. In 834 a Viking fleet sacked

Dorestad, an important trading city in what is now the Netherlands. And seven years later another raiding party sailed up the Seine and attacked Rouen (now in France). In 843 Nantes, on the Loire, was looted, and the Vikings set up a permanent base near the mouth of that river. A similar base appeared a few years later on the island of Oissel, in the Seine.

Meanwhile, another band of Vikings attacked Paris in 845. Charles the Bald, ruler of the western Frankish kingdom, paid them 7,000 pounds (3,157kg) of silver to go away, the first of thirteen Danegolds paid by Frankish leaders between that year and 926. But these payments failed to keep the Vikings out of the region. Some of them established a small kingdom centered on Dorestad in 850, and individual raids continued in the next two decades. A French monk of that period lamented:

A contemporary artist captures the teamwork and raw energy displayed by Viking warriors as they attacked Paris in A.D. 845.

The number of ships grows. The endless stream of Vikings never ceases to increase. Everywhere the Christians are victims of massacres, burnings, plunderings. The Vikings conquer all in their path. . . . Rouen is laid waste . . . Paris, Beauvais, and Meaux taken, Melun's strong fortress leveled to the ground, Chartres occupied . . . and every town besieged.[25]

Though these raids took a toll, the Vikings eventually encountered stiff resistance in the Frankish lands. In the 860s a number of local noblemen organized defensive forces and delivered the intruders a series of sound defeats. And the same thing happened later. The Vikings attacked Paris again in 885, but a local ruler, Count Odo, drove them away from the Seine region four years later. They then tried to conquer Brittany, in western France, but were foiled there as well.

Assaults on England

Although some attacks on Frankish lands continued to occur in the years that followed, the difficulties the Vikings encountered there often motivated them to turn their attentions elsewhere. England was a prime example. At the time, it was not a unified country but rather a collection of small kingdoms, including East Anglia in the east; Northumbria (including York) in the north; Mercia in the middle; and the strongest, Wessex (including London), in the south.

The large Norse force that had appeared on Thanet in 865 rapidly increased in size and became known as the "Great Army" (or "Great Fleet"). In the years that followed it marched northward, southward, and westward, fighting battles and gaining control of large swaths of territory. In 866, *The Anglo-Saxon Chronicle* says, "a large heathen army" arrived. Led by three chiefs—Ivar the Boneless, Halfdan, and Ubbi—the invaders "fixed their winter-quarters in East-Anglia, where they were soon horsed [able to move over land]." The Vikings first went north and invaded Northumbria, where two local rival claimants for the throne temporarily patched up their differences and faced the enemy together. "Having collected a vast force," the English leaders fought the invaders at York. But "there was an immense slaughter of the Northumbrians [and] both the kings were slain on the spot."[26]

With York firmly in their control, the Vikings pushed back into East Anglia and defeated and killed its ruler, King Edmund. Mercia fell to the intruders soon afterward. That left only Wessex, the last unconquered English kingdom, to stand alone against the advancing horde. The Vikings entered Wessex in 878. At first they were successful, and the local king, Alfred, fled with his followers into some impassable marshes. A formidable character in his own right, Alfred built a fortress there from which he struck at the invaders in a series of sneak attacks. Finally he decisively defeated them, forcing them to leave his kingdom. With great relief, the anonymous person then in charge of

King Edmund, ruler of East Anglia, is slain by Vikings. Eventually, the English regrouped, struck back, and defeated the invaders.

the chronicle asserted: "The enemy had not, thank God, entirely destroyed the English nation!"[27]

In 886 Alfred signed a treaty with Viking leaders, who pledged to stay out of Wessex and remain in a large Norse occupation zone stretching across eastern England. The zone became known as the Danelaw.

The English in Wessex were not content to see their fellow Anglo-Saxons suffer under Viking rule, however. After Alfred died in 899, his son and successor Edward the Elder, aided by his capable sister Aethelflaeda (a bold and skilled military leader), launched one campaign after another against the Vikings. The siblings, joined by Edward's own son Athelstan, eventually succeeded in capturing all of the Danelaw. The last Norse holdout was a colorful warrior-chieftain, Erik Bloodaxe, an exiled king of Norway and the final ruler of the Viking kingdom of York. When he was killed in an ambush in 954, the way was open for the rise of a true English nation.

Wessex Resists the Vikings

As recounted in The Anglo-Saxon Chronicle, *in the mid-890s a large Viking army entered Wessex and threatened London. King Alfred blockaded the Lea River, forcing many of the invaders to abandon their ships and depart.*

In the summer [there] went a large party of the citizens [of Wessex] and also of other folk, and made an attack on the work of the Danes [i.e., Vikings]; but they were there routed. [Then] the king [rode] by the river and observed a place where the river might be obstructed, so that they [the Vikings] could not bring out their ships. And they did so. They wrought two works [barricades] on the two sides of the river. [The Vikings had to abandon their ships and depart]. Then rode the king's army westward after the enemy. And the men of London fetched the ships; and all [the ships] that they could not lead away they broke up; but all that were worthy of capture they brought into the port of London.

James Ingram, trans., *The Anglo-Saxon Chronicle*, Online Medieval and Classical Library. http://omacl.org/Anglo/part2.html.

Discouraged by English resistance and victories, many Vikings turned their attention to Ireland, which was more vulnerable. Norse raids in Ireland had done severe damage in the early 800s, but they had noticeably tapered off in the late years of that century. In the 900s Viking fleets once more sailed up Irish rivers and raided deep inland.

From the Mediterranean to the Caspian

While Viking fleets assaulted the English, Franks, Irish, and other western Europeans in the mid-800s, Norse adventurers moved on to southern and eastern Europe and well beyond. In 844 a Viking fleet of more than a hundred ships left the base on the Loire and approached the northern shores of the Iberian Peninsula (now occupied by Spain and Portugal). Defenders of the Christian kingdom of Galicia and Sturias rallied and repelled the attackers, who then sailed southward to the Muslim kingdom of Cordoba. There they sacked Lisbon and Cadiz and sailed up the Guadalquivir River and captured Seville before being defeated by a local Muslim army.

In 857 another Viking fleet from the Loire, this one with sixty-two ships, passed through the Strait of Gibraltar and entered the Mediterranean Sea.

The marauders ravaged the coasts of Morocco (in North Africa) and the Balearic Islands. Three years later they reached Italy, where they sailed up the Arno River and sacked Pisa and Fiesole. On their way home they were defeated by Spanish Muslims once again, and fewer than a third of the original pirate vessels made it back to the Loire.

The Norse were no less active in eastern Europe and western Asia. By 830 they had explored the major components of Russia's vast river system, including the easily navigable Volga, Dnieper, Lovat, and Dvina rivers. They also established strong trade contacts with Arab states south of Russia and the Greek-ruled Byzantine Empire centered in Constantinople, on the southern rim of the Black Sea. The local Slavic peoples called these eastern Vikings the Rus (from which the name *Russia* derives). These were the Vikings whom the Muslim traveler Ibn Fadlan observed up close and wrote about.

As had happened in western Europe, vigorous trade proved a prelude to raiding and attempts at conquest. Sometime in the 850s or 860s a group of Rus established a permanent base near the site of the later city of Novgorod in northwest Russia. Not long afterward, they traveled down the Dnieper River and captured the hilltop town of Kiev,

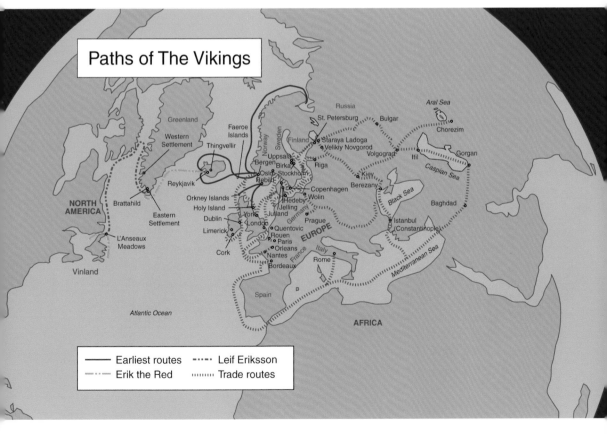

Paths of The Vikings

Earliest routes ···· Leif Eriksson
Erik the Red ⅲⅲⅲ Trade routes

the present-day capital of Ukraine. Kiev became the capital of a large Rus kingdom that eventually stretched from Finland in the north to the Black Sea in the south. The Rus also tried but failed to capture Constantinople and attacked and looted the Muslim lands situated around the Caspian Sea.

Over time most of the Rus settled down as farmers and blended with the local Slavs. A few, however, remained more traditional Viking warriors. Known as the Varangians, or "ax-bearers," they became an elite force within the Byzantine army—the Varangian Guard, charged with protecting the Byzantine emperors.

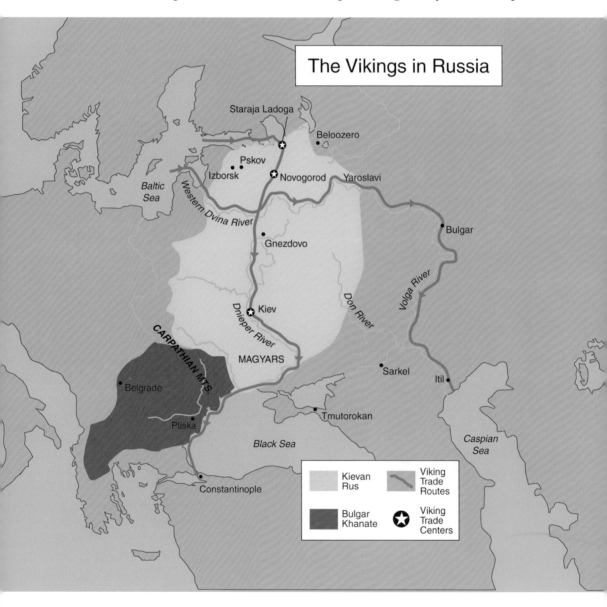

The Vikings in Russia

Staraja Ladoga
Beloozero
Pskov
Izborsk
Novogorod
Yaroslavi
Baltic Sea
Western Dvina River
Bulgar
Gnezdovo
Volga River
Kiev
Don River
Dnieper River
CARPATHIAN MTS.
MAGYARS
Sarkel
Itil
Belgrade
Tmutorokan
Pliska
Black Sea
Caspian Sea
Constantinople

Kievan Rus
Viking Trade Routes
Bulgar Khanate
Viking Trade Centers

Cloaks, Axes, and Tattoos

Impressed by the Vikings he met in what is now Russia, Muslim traveler Ibn Fadlan describes their physical characteristics:

I have never seen more perfect physiques than theirs—they are like palm trees, are fair and reddish. . . . The [Viking] man wears a cloak with which he covers one half of his body, leaving one of his arms uncovered. Every one of them carries an axe, a sword, and a dagger and is never without all of that which we have mentioned. Their swords are of the Frankish variety, with broad, ridged blades. Each man, from the tip of his toes to his neck, is covered in dark-green lines, pictures [tattoos] and such like. Each woman has, on her breast, a small disc, tied around her neck, made of either iron, silver, copper, or gold, in relation to her husband's financial and social worth.

Quoted in James E. Montgomery, "Ibn Fadlan and the Rusiyyah," Cornell University Library. www.library .cornell.edu/colldev/mideast/montgo1.pdf.

The kind of fierce, well-armed Viking warrior witnessed by Ibn Fadlan in Russia is well-illustrated in this colorful modern rendering.

It became a matter of tremendous prestige to serve as a Varangian Guard. The great pride felt by so many Vikings who served in that capacity was captured in a message carved on a boulder found near Stockholm, Sweden: "Ragnvald let the runes be cut. He was in Greece [i.e., served in Constantinople]. He was the leader of the host [the Varangians]."[28] Like members of the U.S. Secret Service who famously pledge to "take a bullet" for the president they guard, the Varangians came to be known for their willingness to die for the emperors. In the early 1100s the Byzantine princess and scholar Anna Comnena described the legendary loyalty of the Varangians:

> [They] bear on their shoulders the heavy iron sword [and] they regard loyalty to the emperors and the protection of their persons as a family tradition, a kind of sacred trust and inheritance handed down from generation to generation. This allegiance they preserve inviolate [never violated] and will never brook [tolerate] the slightest hint of betrayal.[29]

The Norse penetrations into western Asia were part of a larger pattern of exploration, expansion, exploitation, and naked conquest. During the Viking Age, people of Scandinavian birth or lineage attacked or settled in what are now England, Ireland, France, Belgium, the Netherlands, Germany, Spain, Portugal, Morocco, Italy, Greece, Poland, Russia, Armenia, and Iran, among many others. The speed of this burst of expansion and the audacity of its perpetrators awed both the natives of these lands and all future generations. In Wilson's words, Viking civilization "had risen like a star to its zenith—an object of wonder and fear to the world of the succeeding millennium."[30]

Chapter Three

Viking Warriors and Ships

The Norse fought on both land and sea, but no matter where they fought, Viking warriors were essentially foot soldiers, or infantrymen. They utilized basically the same armor and weapons whether fighting in a field or on the deck of a ship. Their equipment was not unusual for its day. In fact, the frequent success of Viking fighters did not derive from some specialized weapon or other unusual device; rather, the vast majority of these warriors used the same armor and weapons as most other medieval European soldiers. Also, there is little or no evidence that Viking fighters were any more skilled with these weapons than other warriors of the age.

What made Viking warriors different, and quite often feared, was their reputation for bravery and fierceness. This status was built partly on the brutal hit-and-run tactics and general lack of mercy they employed in their initial raids on western Europe. Also, their ships were fast and their leaders bold and aggressive. And many of their opponents, particularly those who had never actually seen or fought them before, were put off by the fact that the early Vikings were pagans, which added to their scary image as primitive wild men of the north.

Still another psychological factor that reinforced the image of the fierce Viking warrior was a series of legends about invincible Norse fighters called berserkers. These were supposedly men who, just prior to battle, entered into trancelike states and thereafter fought with a mindless ferocity that made them unstoppable. (This is the source of the English word *berserk*, meaning violently out of control.) In his *Ynglinga Saga*, Snorri Sturluson describes the charge of some berserkers, who "rushed forwards without armor, were as mad as dogs or wolves, bit their shields, and

were strong as bears or wild bulls, and killed people at a blow, but neither fire nor iron told upon [could harm] themselves. These were called Berserker."[31] Most modern experts think that the berserkers' trances and invincibility were legendary and literary exaggerations. Nevertheless, some Viking warriors did call themselves berserkers and thereby helped to perpetuate the fearsome reputation of Norse fighting men.

A Warrior's Defensive Gear

Viking soldiers did not represent major nation-states like the Roman and Byzantine empires, so they did not wear official, standardized uniforms. However, most Vikings dressed in similar fashion, with variations based on family tradition, personal taste, or financial means. To protect the upper body, average warriors donned jerkins (tight jackets without sleeves or collars) made of quilted linen or leather, sometimes with small metal plates sewn into them.

Those who could afford it wore mail, sometimes called chain mail, which was more expensive to buy or make. It consisted of rows of iron rings or scales either riveted or sewn together to form a heavy protective shirt. Such shirts were sometimes called byrnies. Mail was both flexible and strong, but it was by

The well-trained, highly militaristic Vikings could strike almost anywhere without warning. Here, they swarm ashore at Tynemouth, in eastern England.

A modern reenactor shows off a Viking warrior's standard defensive gear, including helmet, chain mail, and shield.

no means foolproof, for while it could deflect a sword's or an arrow's glancing blow, it could not stop a vigorous direct thrust or puncture by such weapons.

To protect the head, Norse fighters wore helmets. However, it is largely a myth that they used double-horned helmets like those so often portrayed in Hollywood movies. Most Viking helmets were actually conical in shape, as explained by noted archaeologist James Graham-Campbell:

> You may search among the contemporary illustrations of Viking warriors from Iceland to Sweden and almost all will be found to show men with pointed heads. A simple conical cap, most probably of leather . . . seems to have been the normal protection for the head of a Viking warrior. The most complete find of an iron helmet is from the grave of a tenth-century Norwegian Viking and consists of a simple rounded cap, made in several pieces, with a spectacle-like guard for the eyes and nose.[32]

Another important defensive device was the shield. Most commonly it was round and about 3 feet (1m) in diameter, with a large metal nub, or boss, protruding from the center of the front. Such a shield was constructed of wood and covered with a sheet of tough leather. Some evidence suggests that the warrior decorated it with designs of his own choosing. His boots were also fashioned of tough cowhide, or else sealskin. He wore a cape or cloak, furlined in the winter, that he pinned at one shoulder or, in some cases, one hip.

Offensive Weapons and Tactics

The chief offensive weapons of Viking soldiers were the sword, ax, spear, and bow and arrow. By the start of the Viking Age, battle-axes had mostly gone out of style in central and southern Europe. The Scandinavians still used them, however, and the Vikings reintroduced them to the rest of Europe for a time. Viking spears were most often made of ash-wood; those meant for throwing were thin and fairly light, while those intended for thrusting were thicker and heavier.

In the vast majority of cases, a Viking's favorite weapon was his sword. Most Norse swords were single-edged in early times, but double-edged swords eventually came into wide use. These weapons were often "treated

Pictured is an array of offensive Norse weapons, including spears and battle-axes.

Special Prearranged Battles

One unusual aspect of warfare among opposing Viking groups was fighting in a so-called "hazelled field," described here by Ian Heath, an expert on medieval warfare:

The hazelled field [was] a specially chosen battlefield, fenced with hazel branches on all sides, where a battle was fought at a prearranged time and date by mutual agreement of the protagonists [opposing sides]. Once challenged to fight in a hazelled field, it was apparently a dishonor to refuse, or to ravage your opponent's territory until after the battle had been fought. . . . The latest reference to such a hazelled field that I am aware of dates to 978, when Earl Hakon Sigurdsson of Norway defeated King Ragnfrid (one of Erik Bloodaxe's sons) in a field marked out with hoslur [hazel branches].

Ian Heath, *The Vikings*. Oxford, Eng.: Osprey, 2001, pp. 32, 45.

with a certain amount of reverence," scholar Ian Heath points out,

especially in the case of old swords that had been handed down from generation to generation or looted from burial mounds. A certain mystique clung to such weapons, which were usually given high-sounding names such as "Byrnie-biter," "Long-and-sharp," and "Golden-hilted." The very best swords were imported from the Frankish kingdoms, though Viking craftsmen usually fitted them with ornate hilts and grips of metal, bone, horn, and walrus ivory.[33]

These weapons were effective enough when used on an individual opponent in an informal, spontaneous military situa-tion, such as a raid. But they were even more formidable in the more formal setting of a pitched battle. The number of fighters Viking leaders fielded for such battles was usually in the hundreds and only occasionally a few thousand.

Such a unit could do serious damage when it employed its most common offensive tactic—the shield-wall. This was a massive formation in which the soldiers stood in ranks (rows), one behind the other. Usually there were five or more ranks, with the better-armed men stationed in the front two ranks. These men raised their shields, which were touching, or even overlapping, and marched forward at the enemy. Only after they had made contact and sent their opponents reeling backward did they break ranks and fight individually. The ninth-century Oseberg tapestry, excavated in southern Norway in 1904, shows part of such a shield-wall. And one is mentioned in *King Harald's Saga*—a part of Snorri Sturluson's *Heimskringla*—in the section describing the battle of Stamford Bridge, against an English army: "Then King Harald arranged his army, and made the line of battle long, but not deep. He bent both wings of it back, so that they met together; and formed a wide ring equally thick all round, shield to shield, both in the front and rear ranks."[34]

Thus, the Vikings fought almost exclusively on foot. Unlike the Franks, who

The ranks of a medieval Viking shield wall are accurately reproduced by modern reeanctors. Such formations often had five or more ranks.

were known for their cavalry units (horse-mounted fighters), the Norse rarely, if ever, trained horses for use in battle. Most often, Heath says, "they used horses simply as a means of increasing their mobility during their raiding expeditions. They either rounded up horses for this purpose in the vicinity of their encampment, or took those of a defeated enemy after a battle."[35]

The Sleek, Fast Longships

The Vikings were far more comfortable in ships than they were on horses. In fact, in the Viking Age their ships were among the finest in Europe and quite literally made their successes in trade, raiding, warfare, and exploration possible. These vessels evolved from the large rowboats mentioned by the first-century Roman historian Tacitus in his descriptions of the Scandinavians of his day. He made the point that they had no sails. Archaeologists unearthed the remains of some boats of this type in a bog in southern Denmark in the 1800s. Called Nydam ships (after the town in which they were found), they were propelled strictly by oars and were suitable mainly for travel on rivers and along local coastlines.

Later, improved construction and the addition of masts and sails resulted in the sleek, fast vessels that allowed the Vikings to range far and wide across Europe and well beyond. The general Norse term for such a ship, which benefited from a combination of sail and oar power, was *langskip,* or "longship." A number of different types existed.

One, the *threttensessa,* had twenty-six oars (thirteen on each side). Longships with forty to fifty-six oars were called *snekkja.* And those having still more oars were known as *skei* or *drekar* ("dragons"). The building of one of these large dragons in about the year 1000 is mentioned in *King Olaf Tryg-gvasson's Saga:*

> Thorberg Skafhog was the man's name who was the master-builder of the ship; but there were many others besides,—some to fell wood, some to shape it, some to make nails, some to carry timber; and all that was used was of the best. The ship was both long and broad and high-sided, and strongly timbered. In the evening the king went out, and Thorberg with him, to see how the vessel looked, and everybody said that never was seen so large and so beautiful a ship of war. . . . The king called this ship Serpent the Long. [It] had thirty-four benches for rowers [on each side]. This ship was the best and most costly ship ever made in Norway.[36]

A slightly larger warship, with thirty-five rowers on a side, was constructed in 1062 by the Viking leader Harald (Sigurdsson) Hardrada. He called it the *Great Dragon.* Naming these vessels after powerful animals, both real and mythical, was the standard custom. The object was to underscore the power of the ships themselves. Other examples included *Fjord Elk, Surf Dragon,* and *Oar Steed.*

The Better Shipbuilder

In this excerpt from the saga of Norway's King Olaf, the shipbuilder Thorberg Skafhog sees that the king's new ship is being poorly constructed and points it out by sabotaging the work:

Early next morning the king returned again to the ship, and Thorberg with him. The carpenters were there before them, but all were standing idle with their arms across. The king asked, "What is the matter?" They said [that] somebody had gone from stem to stern and cut one deep notch after the other down the one side of the planking. [The king] said, "The man shall die who has thus destroyed the vessel.". . . "I can tell you, king," said Thorberg, "who has done this piece of work. . . . I did it myself." The king said, "You must restore it all to the same condition as before, or your life shall pay for it." Then Thorberg went and chipped the planks until the deep notches were all smoothed [and] the king and all present declared that the ship was much handsomer on the side of the hull which Thorberg had chipped, and bade him shape the other side in the same way; and gave him great thanks for the improvement. Afterwards Thorberg was the master builder of the ship until she was entirely finished.

Snorri Sturluson, *Heimskringla*, Project Gutenberg. www.gutenberg.org/files/598/598-h/598-h.htm# 2H_4_0204.

Construction of a Longship

The manner in which Viking ships were built can be seen by examining the remains of some that have been excavated in the past two centuries.

Perhaps the most famous is the so-called Gokstad ship, found in Norway in 1880. The hull was made of oak, selected for its hardness and stability, while the planks making up the deck, the mast, and the oars were made of pine. To cut and fashion these wooden parts, the builders used metal axes and saws, sharp knives, and chisels.

The initial construction step was to carve the keel, the spinelike, T-shaped piece of wood running lengthwise along the bottom of the hull. Joined to each end of the keel was a piece of wood that curved upward, becoming the prow in the front and the stern in the rear. Meanwhile, along the central section of the keel a number of wooden ribs curved upward. The hull boards, or strakes, were attached to these ribs. Each strake overlapped the one below it, a method called "clinkering."

The deck area of the Gokstad ship featured deck planks held together by iron nails. There were also wooden benches for the rowers and a pine mast 33 feet (10m) high. Evidence shows that

The famous Gokstad ship, discovered in 1880, was partially reconstructed in the Viking Ship Museum in Oslo, Norway.

the sail was 36 feet (11m) across and made of white wool with sewn-on red stripes. When this sail was in use, it likely allowed the vessel to attain a speed of up to 20 knots (23 miles per hour; 37km/h). Probably the sail was employed mainly for voyages in the open sea, while the oars were used mostly for travel along the coastlines.

Navigation was of course easiest along the coastlines, where captains and crews could use sightings of various landmarks on shore for guidance. It was a very different story when they were out in the open sea and out of sight of land. According to Haywood:

> Though they lacked the magnetic compass, the Vikings possessed a simple sun compass which could locate north with tolerable accuracy in clear weather. Viking navigators could also use the stars to judge latitude, a great aid to navigation if the latitude of the destination was known. [In addition] navigators would have been heirs to a stock of orally transmitted practical knowledge of sea and weather conditions.[37]

Longships in Battle

Although Viking longships were employed for ordinary travel and for voyages of exploration, they are perhaps most famously known for their use in warfare. Their most common wartime application was ferrying warriors to and from the sites of land-based raids or battles. However, longships also took direct part in sea battles, mostly fought between rival Viking groups.

Because they were essentially foot soldiers, Norse fighters sought to make their sea battles as much like land battles as possible. To this end, once the rival groups had reached the site of combat, each side lowered their sails and lashed several of their own vessels together, creating a large floating platform. The chief strategy was to land one's warriors on the enemy's platform and defeat that enemy in hand-to-hand fighting. If victory was achieved, the winners cut the opposing ships loose and either sank them or kept them for their own use.

A few such sea battles were described in the Icelandic sagas. The following passage from King Olaf's saga in Sturluson's *Heimskringla* describes the climax of the battle of Svölder, which occurred in the western Baltic Sea circa 1000. Olaf, then king of Norway, led a fleet of eleven ships to oppose an alliance of foes, including the kings of Denmark and Sweden, who had at least seventy ships. The attackers,

Viking ships clash in a battle fought between rival groups of Norse. Such encounters featured a great deal of hand-to-hand combat.

Ships with Perfect Bottoms

In the early 1890s, a group of modern Viking ship enthusiasts constructed a replica of the Gokstad ship, a medieval vessel discovered a few years earlier. They named the replica the Viking *and sailed it across the Atlantic Ocean. The ship's captain, Magnus Anderson, later wrote:*

We often had the pleasure of darting through the water at speeds of 10 and sometimes even 11 knots [11.5 to 12.6 miles per hour]. Whether the old Norsemen used their ships in the same way as this is hard to say, but it does not seem unlikely that they used the ships for all they were worth. It seems absolutely certain that in those days too they wished to travel as fast as possible. Why else should they have taken the trouble to improve the structure until it was so perfect that not even the shipbuilders of our time can do better as far as the ship's bottom is concerned. The fact is that the finest merchant-ships of our day . . . have practically the same type of bottom as the Viking ships.

Quoted in David M. Wilson, *The Vikings and Their Origins*. London: Thames and Hudson, 2001, p. 78.

having defeated Olaf's fleet and taken all his ships, boarded his flagship, the *Serpent*, and attempted to capture the king:

Now the fight became hot indeed, and many men fell on board the Serpent. . . . So many men of the Serpent had fallen, that the ship's sides were in many places quite bare of defenders; and the earl's men poured in all around into the vessel, and all the men who were still able to defend the ship crowded aft to the king, and arrayed themselves for his defense. [One witness recalled that] the gallant few of Olaf's crew must take refuge on the quarter-deck. Around the king they stand in [a] ring. Their shields enclose the king from foes, and the few who still remain fight madly, but in vain.[38]

Such maritime encounters among the Norse proved to be the height of naval warfare in Europe's early medieval era. It was not until well after the close of the Viking Age that the advent of naval artillery (cannons aboard ships) made sea battles more destructive and lethal.

Chapter Four

Viking Families and Home Life

Most modern depictions of the Vikings show them dressed in war gear and engaged in raids or other violent activities. Few portray their towns, homes, and families back in Scandinavia, where most were farmers, craftsmen, merchants, and/or traders who rarely or never went to war. Indeed, evidence indicates that the vast majority of Vikings had largely peaceful lives and occupations. Very much like most people today, their main priority was to create economically prosperous and comfortable homes for themselves and their families. As one historian puts it, throughout the Viking Age

there remained at home in Scandinavia farmers, hunters, fishermen, and trappers who led the same lives as their forebears. It was those who stayed at home who provided the resources that made the voyages

practicable. The ships had to be built, equipped, and provisioned. Supplies had to be accumulated for the winter months, and so had the commodities required to make up the cargoes of the traders. No true picture of the Vikings and their achievements can be gained without some understanding of their economic [and social] background in Scandinavia.[39]

Typical Houses

The center of economic and family life in early medieval Scandinavia was the home, which in many cases was quite large and comfortable. From the standpoint of both looks and construction, houses differed considerably from one region to another. In those days, for instance, Denmark had large stands of hardwood forests, so the locals took advantage of this fact and built their homes primarily from hardwood boards and posts. Farther north, in Norway and Sweden, people had access to vast pine forests. The pine trees often had very straight trunks. And because pine is a soft wood, they were easy to cut, so log cabins similar to those in the early American frontier became common. In time the Vikings settled Iceland, which, unlike Scandinavia, had few forests. As a result, the Icelanders came to build their houses from field stones and mounds of earth. Some Viking farmers chose still another approach to house construction, called wattle-and-daub. They first dug a pit. Around its edges they raised the walls, which consisted of wattle (interwoven tree branches) smeared with daub (clay, plaster, or dung). The ceiling was composed of thatch, thickly interwoven branches and straw.

Whatever the manner of their construction, most houses in the Viking lands had similar interiors. Usually, a house had a big central hall, or living room, which University of Wisconsin scholar Kirsten Wolf describes this way:

The fire was on a slightly raised, stone-lined hearth. [The] fire was fed with peat or wood kept outside the house. . . . Some houses had a small oven or roasting pit against the wall instead of, or in addition to, an open hearth. The ovens were made on a framework of wattle and shaped like a dome. [Meanwhile] raised platforms along the walls of the house served as seats and beds close to the fire, though for sleeping accommodation some houses had built-in

These modern reconstructions of Viking houses employ the wattle-and-daub technique, topped by roofs of thatch.

A reconstructed interior of a Viking house includes wood paneling and several raised platforms, the latter used for sleeping, storage, and work-benches.

closets, which provided at least some privacy. Presumably, these platforms were covered with furs, skins, or woolen blankets. [The] walls appear to have been wainscoted [paneled with wood], and in some houses the panels were adorned with incised carving or woven hangings or tapestries.[40]

Usually the raised platforms in a house were the only furniture, though some of the larger, richer homes had individual beds and/or chairs, along with wooden chests for storage. These bigger houses also featured two or three extra chambers, used either as workrooms or private bedrooms, attached to the main one. However many rooms a house had, it had few or no windows so as to keep warmth from escaping. As a result, a typical home must have reeked from a combination of smoke from the hearth, burning fat from oil lamps (the only source of light besides the hearth), human body odors, and animal fur and dung (because people often kept their animals in the house in cold weather). The smell of human wastes was fortunately not part of the mix, as members of the family relieved themselves in small wooden outhouses situated outside.

An aerial view of reconstructed sod houses at L'Anse aux Meadows shows the type of outer fence that Norse farmers typically used to coral their goats, cattle, and other livestock.

Farming and Trade

A good many Viking houses were located in towns, which were most often built near the seashore or along rivers or fjords (long, bay-like inlets from the sea). But many other homes were erected on farms, which dotted the landscape wherever Viking groups settled. The kind of farming in which these groups engaged depended on the area in which they dwelled. In Norway and Sweden, where small pockets of arable land were widely separated by mountains, glaciers, and fjords, few crops were raised. The chief economic activity was livestock raising (or animal husbandry). Nearly everyone in these regions raised cattle, pigs, goats,

and sheep. In Denmark, by contrast, farmers had these same animals, but in addition they had enough good land to grow large amounts of rye, barley, oats, peas, cabbage, and beans. Meanwhile, most Scandinavians continued to supplement their diets with hunting and fishing.

Although many Norse were farmers of one sort or another, making a living from farming alone was often difficult. With the exception of parts of Denmark, rich, arable land was scarce in Scandinavia, and the climate was frequently harsh for a large portion of the year. So it was common to supplement one's farming activities with other economic activities. Raiding was one option that some men took, of course. But far more chose to engage in some form of trade.

One such farmer-trader whose exploits have survived in written accounts was Ohthere (or Ottar), a local chief who dwelled in Halogaland, in northern Norway, in the late 800s. In an account he passed on to others, he explained that he had no more than twenty cows, twenty sheep, and twenty pigs. His soil, which he plowed using a horse, was poor, so he hunted reindeer and walrus and traded bear and otter skins to help make ends meet. Like the Vikings who went raiding, Ohthere was in large degree dependent on the sea because to exchange his goods he periodically had to sail to small trading centers scattered across Norway and Denmark. Describing some of these travels and the landmarks he looked for, he wrote:

There is a port to the south of this land, which is called Sciringes-heal. [A] man could not sail [there] in a month, if he watched into the night, and every day had a fair wind; and all the while he shall sail along the coast; and on his right hand first is Island, then the islands which are between Island and this land. Then this land continues quite to Sciringes-heal; and all the way on the left is Norway. To the south of Sciringes-heal a great sea runs up a vast way into the country, and is so wide that no man can see across it.[41]

Ohthere traded animal hides, furs, and meat, along with whatever other valuable products he could get his hands on. Other part- or full-time Viking traders dealt in the products of various crafts, among

Viking Drinks

Among the most popular drinks of the Scandinavian Vikings were milk (from both cattle and goats) and whey. The latter is the liquid left over when milk curdles and the solids are strained out. Whey could be drunk by itself or mixed with other liquids. The Norse also drank alcoholic beverages, including wine, ale, and beer, usually served in wooden cups, silver bowls, or hollow cattle horns. An old Viking proverb about beer has survived and says: "Praise not the day until evening has come; a woman until she is burnt; a sword until it is tried; a maiden until she is married; ice until it has been crossed; beer until it has been drunk."

Quoted in *Brookstone Beer Bulletin*, "Beer Quotations." http://brookstonbeerbulletin.com/beer-quotations.

them metalworking (including making swords, axes, and jewelry), tanning, woodworking, and shipbuilding. Still others traded precious metals such as silver and gold and, when they were available from foreign raids, slaves.

Women and Marriage

However a Viking man supported his family, that family was most often nuclear. That is, like average modern families, it consisted of a father, mother, and their children. Extended families featuring grandparents, aunts, cousins, and so forth were far less common in Viking society. "The reason," Wolf points out, is that "the average life expectancy was somewhere between 30 and 40 years at most, and only a small percentage of people lived long enough to enter the role of grandparent."[42]

As a rule, the father, husband, or other chief male present was the head of a Viking household. When he was away trading or raiding (or was deceased), however, his wife or mother assumed control of the family. Even when the leading male was in the house, the average Viking woman was frequently as tough, capable, and hardworking as he was. She raised the children, cleaned, made the family clothes, cooked the meals, and instructed her daughters in how to perform these duties. Moreover, it was not unusual for women to grab weapons and fight alongside the men when their community was in peril.

Indeed, evidence suggests that many Viking women, especially widows whose sons were already grown, were quite independent and commanded a certain amount of respect and social power within the community. Of several notable women described in the Icelandic sagas, the most famous example is that of Unn (sometimes called Aud) the Deepminded, wife of a Norse king of Dublin. In about the year 900 her husband and son were slain in battle, and she was left in charge of several grandchildren. Feeling that they were not safe in Ireland, Unn decided to move them to Iceland. According to the *Laxdoela Saga*:

> She had a ship built secretly in the forest. When it was finished, she made the ship ready and set out with substantial wealth. She took along all her kinsmen who were still alive, and people say it is hard to find another example of a woman managing to escape from such a hostile situation with as much wealth and as many followers. It shows what an outstanding woman Unn was. [Later] she traveled through all the valleys of Breidafjord [in western Iceland] and took as much land as she wished.[43]

The fact that Unn went on to claim a large tract of vacant land in Iceland and later divided it up and gave parcels to various relatives is revealing. It shows that under certain circumstances Norse women could own and bequeath land just as men could. It is unknown how many women were as assertive and capable as Unn, but most scholars agree

Modern reenactors, clad in authentic outfits, engage in some of the typical duties performed by Viking women, including food preparation and yarn-spinning.

Viking Families and Home Life ■ 59

with Wolf's speculation that "the resourcefulness and independence exhibited by Unn and others may well have been fostered by the many responsibilities with which women were left when their husbands were away on trading voyages and military expeditions."[44]

One social area in which women did not have much say was marriage. In Viking society marriage was a largely social and legal contract in which romantic love played little or no role. A typical marriage was arranged. The suitor or his father (or both) approached the bride's father and made the arrangements, including those regarding the dowry (money or other valuables supplied by the girl's father for her maintenance in the marriage). The wedding consisted of a feast that took place at the groom's house or bride's father's house.

Varied and Nutritious Foods

Whether at a wedding feast or an ordinary daily meal, the foods consumed by the members of Viking families were both varied and nutritious. One common staple was bread made from barley or wheat. A mention of such bread appears in a Norse poem, the *Rigspula*, along with other hearty food items:

Then took Mother a figured cloth, white, of linen, and covered the

Always Be Polite

This speech, preserved in the medieval Norwegian document titled The King's Mirror, *is by a Norse father instructing his son on how to be civil in certain situations. Here, the father cites the polite rules of marketplaces and other places where large numbers of people gathered.*

When you are in a market town, or wherever you are, be polite and agreeable; then you will secure the friendship of all good men. Make it a habit to rise early in the morning, and go first and immediately to church. . . . When the services are over, go out to look after your business affairs. If you are unacquainted with the traffic of the town, observe carefully how those who are reputed the best and most prominent merchants conduct their business. You must also be careful to examine the wares that you buy before the purchase is finally made to make sure that they are sound and flawless. And whenever you make a purchase, call in a few trusty men to serve as witnesses as to how the bargain was made.

Laurence M. Larson, trans., *The King's Mirror*. www.mediumaevum.com/75years/mirror/sec1.html#V.

board [table]; thereafter took she a fine-baked loaf, white of wheat and covered the cloth. Next she brought forth plenteous dishes, set with silver, and spread the board with brown-fried bacon and roasted birds. There was wine in a vessel and rich-wrought goblets. They drank and reveled while day went by.[45]

The "roasted birds" mentioned in the passage included chickens, ducks, and geese. The Vikings enjoyed a wide range of other meats as well, among them pork, lamb, goat, deer, elk, rabbit, bear, seal, and whale. (Oil from the seals was also used as fuel for lamps and as an alternative to tar in weatherproofing boat hulls.)

Fruits and vegetables were frequently on the menu, too, when seasonally available. They included onions, cabbage, peas, garlic, cherries, plums, wild apples, elderberries, and blackberries. The principal food sweetener in the Viking lands was honey.

Viking Burials

The responsibilities of the heads of Viking households included not only supplying a roof over family members' heads and feeding them but also ensuring that they had proper funerals. The dead in Norse society were either cremated (burned) or inhumed (buried), depending on custom in local areas. After the body or ashes were covered over with earth, the grave site was marked by a mound, one or more stones (sometimes carved), or wooden posts.

The now famous and often spectacular "Viking funerals" involving cremation inside full-sized ships were reserved for noted warriors or leaders. In the year 922 the Muslim traveler Ibn Fadlan witnessed such a funeral staged for a Viking chief on the shores of the Baltic Sea. Fadlan said that the dead man's body was placed on a raised platform on a Viking ship. Then the kinfolk erected a canopy over the platform for ten days while they finished making and sewing his funeral garments.

In the meantime, a female slave belonging to the dead man was selected to be sacrificed along with him. "On the day when he and the slave-girl were to be burned," Fadlan wrote, "I arrived at the river where his ship was. To my surprise, I discovered that it had been beached and that four planks of birch and other types of wood had been erected for it. Around them wood had been placed in such a way as to resemble scaffolding."[46]

Then an old woman called the "angel of Death" led the slave girl to the ship, had her drink some special alcoholic brew, and took her inside the canopy. Fadlan continued:

They laid her down beside her master and two of them took hold of her feet, two her hands. The [old woman] placed a rope around her neck in such a way that the ends crossed one another and handed it to two of the men to pull on it. She advanced with a broad-bladed dagger and began to thrust it in and out between her ribs,

Climax of a Viking Burial

In his detailed account of the customs of the Vikings he encountered in Russia, Muslim traveler Ibn Fadlan describes the funeral of a Viking chief. This excerpt tells what happened after the body of a slain slave girl was placed near that of the chief on the funeral pyre.

Then the deceased's next of kin approached and took hold of a piece of wood and set fire to it. . . . He ignited the wood that had been set up under the ship after they had placed the slave-girl whom they had killed beside her master. Then the people came forward with sticks and firewood. Each one carried a stick the end of which he had set fire to and which he threw on top of the wood. The wood caught fire, and then the ship, the pavilion, the man, the slave-girl and all it contained. A dreadful wind arose and the flames leapt higher and blazed fiercely . . . it took scarcely an hour for the ship, the firewood, the slave-girl and her master to be burnt to a fine ash.

Quoted in James E. Montgomery, "Ibn Fadlan and the Rusiyyah," Cornell University Library. www.library .cornell.edu/colldev/mideast/montgo1.pdf.

At the height of the funeral of a Viking chief, the ship containing his body is set afire by his kinsmen and followers.

now here, now there, while the two men throttled her with the rope until she died.[47]

Finally, they burned the ship with the two bodies in it. Archaeologists have confirmed that such elaborate funerals for well-to-do Vikings did occur sometimes. The remnants of one such ceremony were uncovered in 1903 at Oseberg, Norway. They remain a testament to a medieval individual who desired to leave life as boldly and colorfully as he had lived it.

Chapter Five

Viking Communities and Culture

Various Europeans who suffered the violence and indignity of Viking raids and invasions portrayed their attackers as barbarians with no sense of community, decency, or justice. Yet the Vikings were far from lawless, antisocial savages. True, some Norse went raiding to acquire easy access to gold, silver, and other valuables, as well as enhanced reputations, and they often showed little or no mercy to the foreigners they encountered in the raids. But when they returned to their homes in Denmark, Norway, and Sweden, the marauders generally resumed their places in a society with well-ordered villages (and eventually towns); social classes and political organizations; laws, with penalties for those who broke them; and cultural and economic pursuits, including expertise in a wide range of crafts and even writing.

Towns and Social Classes

Part of the evidence for the high degree of organization and efficiency in Viking society can be seen in the excavated remains of towns. Before the advent of the Viking Age, Scandinavia had only small villages, but around the year 800 a few towns—each having between one and two thousand inhabitants—began to appear. One of the earliest, Hedeby, on the southern edge of the Jutland peninsula, was laid out with considerable forethought and orderliness, with streets forming a grid pattern and land plots of more or less standardized size. As Graham-Campbell points out, this suggests the existence of both a strong central authority and a citizenry used to—and willing to follow—set social rules and expectations:

> The fact that the streets were laid out at right angles and parallel to the [nearby] stream, and that the building plots seem to have been regulated in size, indicates a strong urban control . . . from the beginning of Hedeby's existence. . . .

Houses in Hedeby's central settlement were built a little back from, but facing, the streets. They were rectangular, measuring on average about 20 feet by 50 feet (6m by 15m).[48]

The high level of town planning and cooperation among the residents is also shown by various examples of community infrastructure and frequent upkeep. The dirt streets were covered by wooden planks laid out in long, neat rows. And somewhat narrower planked walkways ran at right angles from the streets to the houses' front doors. These wooden pathways not only made walking and pulling carts easier but also largely eliminated the problem of muddy feet in rainy weather. Other examples of communal facilities included shipyards and docks, barns for food storage, local blacksmith forges, and tall mounds of earth and wooden fences to keep the town's outer perimeter safe from attack.

The physical orderliness of the towns and their layout was paralleled to a certain degree by a strict pecking order within Norse society. At the top of the social hierarchy, or ladder of social classes, was the king. Each of the many small Viking kingdoms that rose and fell both inside and outside of Scandinavia in the ninth and tenth centuries had a local strongman with the title of king. Over time, the richest of these

Modern archaeologists excavate a section of the Norse settlement at Hedeby, one of the chief trading centers of the Viking lands.

A reconstruction accurately depicts what a large Norse trading center looked like circa A.D. *800 to 1000.*

rulers had royal courts with considerable finery, pomp, and rules of protocol. Although written shortly after the close of the Viking Age, the Norwegian document known as *The King's Mirror* captures some of the royal codes of behavior:

[When arriving at court] you [should] come fully dressed in good apparel, the smartest that you have, and wearing fine trousers and shoes. You must not come without your coat; and also wear a mantle, the best that you have. For trousers always select cloth of a brown dye. . . . Your shirt should be short, and all your linen rather light. Your shirt should be cut somewhat shorter than your coat. . . . Before you enter the royal presence be sure to have your hair and beard carefully trimmed according to the fashions of the court when you join the same. . . . Now when you seem to be in proper state to appear before the king both as to dress and other matters, and if you come at a suitable time and have permission from the doorkeeper to enter, you must have your coming planned in such a way that some capable servant can accompany you. [But] do not let him follow you farther than inside the door. . . . Leave your mantle behind when you go before the king and be careful to have your hair brushed smooth, and your beard combed with care. You must have neither hat nor cap nor other covering on your head; for one must ap-

pear before lords with uncovered head and ungloved hands, [with] limbs and body thoroughly bathed.[49]

Directly beneath the king on the social ladder were his nobles, the jarls (Old Norse for "earls"). Usually they were local chieftains and/or men who came from well-to-do, highly respected families and served in high positions in local government. Below the jarls, and making up the bulk of Viking society, were the freemen, or *bóndi*. They were mostly farmers, merchants, and craftsmen of average or lower-than-average means. They could bear arms and speak in local assemblies (groups of citizens that met on a regular basis to discuss community matters). Those freemen who became successful traders or raiders achieved higher social status and had a better chance of obtaining good land than did ordinary *bóndi*; thus, at least some chance for upward mobility did exist in Norse society.

The lowest rung on the social ladder was occupied by slaves, or thralls. They became slaves either by being captured in raids or battles or by going bankrupt and offering to serve a master in order to survive. The latter route to slavery was both the least common and most shameful and embarrassing one. One could also be born into slavery because a slave's offspring was also seen as a slave. Slaves could earn their freedom through hard work and loyalty or a variety of other ways. But a freed slave, or freedman, still owed certain services (such as running errands and doing various other favors) to the family of his or her former master.

Government, Laws, and Justice

Members of all the social classes, with the exception of slaves, could take part in some aspect of government. The king was technically the head of a local government and was expected to do what was right for the people, including making sure that justice was served. According to *The King's Mirror*:

> His chief business [is] to maintain an intelligent government and to seek good solutions for all the difficult problems and demands which come before him. And you shall know of a truth that it is just as much the king's duty to observe daily the rules of the sacred law and to preserve justice in holy judgments as it is the bishop's duty to preserve the order of the sacred mass.[50]

It would have been difficult for a Norse king to become a ruthless dictator, because many of his important decisions had to be approved by an assembly of freemen. Such an assembly was called a *thing*. Essentially a big meeting, it was held in the open air once, twice, or several times a year, depending on local custom. There were small-scale, town-level *things*, which dealt with land rights, local construction projects, and disputes among neighbors. Larger, regional-level *things* handled more important matters, such as choosing a king if the old one had died or deciding the region's defensive policies. Of all the Viking lands, only Iceland had a national-level assembly (the Althing).

One of the several functions of a *thing* was to deal with legal matters. First, at some point during the meeting an elected official known as the Lawspeaker read aloud a portion of the local laws. (In Iceland it was a third of the laws.) Then, a person could come forward and accuse someone else of wrongdoing. There were no lawyers, police, or other formal legal personnel, so the accuser prosecuted the case himself, and the accused ran his own defense. The accuser called witnesses to back up his charge. And the accused could and often did call a number of character witnesses to testify that he was of good character and therefore likely innocent. In a minority of cases, the accused endured an ordeal. For example, he might carry a hot iron from one point to another, and if he suffered no burns he was proclaimed innocent.

If the members of the *thing* found the accused guilty, punishment was meted out. The Vikings had no prisons like those in modern societies. Instead, convicted criminals most often paid a fine. This system not only satisfied the accuser, since he received tangible compensation for his losses, it also reduced the level of violence in Norse society. Any disputes that could not be settled in this civilized manner could result in the accuser and accused fighting a duel

A woman accuses a man of wrong-doing in a local thing. *Dealing with legal disputes was only one of several communal functions of a Viking* thing.

to the death. Another common custom (one the justice system sought to avoid), consisted of the accuser's family exacting blood vengeance by killing one or more members of the accused person's family.

If the local society viewed a crime as particularly heinous, the guilty person might be branded an outlaw. Murder, for instance, might result in outlawry (although sometimes the *thing* instead imposed a heavy fine for murder). It was forbidden for anyone to give aid or shelter to an outlaw, even a member of his own family; also, it was perfectly acceptable for anyone to kill an outlaw on sight. In some Viking lands, including Iceland, outlawry was the ultimate punishment. In others, including parts of Denmark, a guilty person could receive the death penalty. Common forms of execution included hanging, burning, stoning, drowning, and burying alive.

Writing and Education

Another indication that the Norse were a civilized people was the fact that both before and during the Viking Age they possessed writing. It was at first based on a rudimentary set of characters called the runic alphabet, which seems to have emerged somewhere in Germany in the second century A.D. Initially it featured twenty-four characters, or runes. But in Scandinavia, by the 800s the number of runes had been reduced to sixteen. Most of the characters consisted of vertical or diagonal lines to make it easier to carve them with the grain on wooden surfaces.

It is unknown whether average Vikings were literate in runes or whether the ability to read and write was reserved to a small literate class. No formal schools existed in Scandinavia during the Viking Age, so reading and writing must have been passed from parents or other adult relatives to children in the home. What is more certain is that runic characters have been found on public monuments, weapons, tools, jewelry, and stone markers beside roads and bridges, as well as in graffiti on tavern walls. (An example of the latter is a message from a worried wife to her drunk husband: "Gyda says that you are to go home!"[51] These facts at least suggest, as Kirsten Wolf says, "that they were intended to be seen and read, and by extension, that a good number, if not the majority, of Viking Age Scandinavians were able to interpret runes."[52]

In the last years of the Viking Age, especially between 1000 and 1100, when many Norse converted to Christianity, they adopted the Roman alphabet. For a while, runic characters coexisted with the new alphabet. Royal edicts and legal and religious texts came to be written in Latin, while everyday writings continued to be expressed in runes. Once Christianity had become the norm, shortly after the end of the Viking Age, formal schools began to appear. Some schools were in monasteries and others were in private homes.

Leisure Activities

As has been true of nearly all peoples in history, Viking cultural traditions were to a considerable degree ex-

Glima's Distinct Movements

Noted modern martial arts researcher and instructor Pete Kautz provides these key facts about the Viking wrestling style of Glima, which is still practiced in Iceland today:

Glima is traditionally practiced outdoors in appropriate clothing for the weather. In Iceland, one of the reasons you might have decided to play a few rounds was just to stay warm on a cold night! These often cold and slippery conditions are part of what goes into giving Glima its distinct movement. It would be practiced on the hillsides or in any natural place that gave shelter, and these were referred to as Glimuholl or literally "Glima Hall." The basic idea is to grip your opponent in the proper way, and then force them to touch their torso or any area above the elbows or knees, to the ground for the best 2 out of 3 falls. Also, if both of their arms touch the ground it is a fall. If both players fall together it is called a "brother-fall" and neither player gets the point. Perhaps the most immediately discernible characteristic of modern Glima is that the participants today wear special leather belts. [These] belts allow a specific grip to be taken. . . . The belt gives something to grab, and it is fair to all competitors.

Pete Kautz, "The Gripping History of Glima," *Journal of Western Martial Art*, January 2000. http://ejmas .com/jwma/articles/2000/jwmaart_kautz_0100.htm.

Icelandic wrestlers, like these photographed in about 1950, continue to practice traditional styles of Glima, as their Viking ancestors did.

These Norse runes were found on a stone in Maes Howe, in Scotland's Orkney Islands.

pressed in the leisure activities in which people engaged. These can be conveniently divided into indoor and outdoor pursuits. Of the indoor variety, board games were popular, including a checkers-like game called Morels, which featured polished stones for playing pieces. Another favorite board game was Hnefatafl, or "King's Table."

It appears to have been similar in some ways to chess.

The Vikings also enjoyed feasts and the parties that accompanied them. In addition to plenty of delicious food and intoxicating drinks, including beer, entertainment was offered. It might have consisted of singing and dancing. Often young boys staged mock battles with wooden swords and shields while the adults cheered on the youngsters. Most popular of all, however, was storytelling. Every village had at least one or two residents, usually middle-aged or elderly, who knew all the myths about the gods and human heroes of old and were skilled in reciting these tales. Occasionally, extremely accomplished poets and storytellers called skalds would entertain the rich, chieftains, and/or the royal courts by reciting poetry. Other poets and storytellers made a comfortable living traveling from town to town and performing for local audiences.

Of the outdoor activities admired in the Viking lands, those related to fighting and warfare were especially popular. They included archery tournaments, spear-throwing contests, and wrestling. Several wrestling styles were accepted, including one called Glima, which featured moves similar to those in modern judo, and a cruder kind in which choking and tripping were allowed. The Vikings also played ballgames, the most popular of which was *knattleikr*. The exact manner in which it was played is uncertain, but evidently it was a team sport in which a player used a bat to hit

Viking Songs

It appears that the skalds and other Norse storytellers supplemented their recitations with music. This is not surprising considering that most or all Vikings enjoyed singing and listening to music. Sailors sang songs while rowing ships, for example, and many farmers sang or hummed tunes while planting or harvesting their crops. In addition, people of all walks of life sang drinking songs at parties. It evidently did not matter much to the average Viking whether or not he, she, or a friend possessed a pleasant singing voice. On the other hand, foreigners exposed to Norse music were sometimes appalled at what they heard. An Arab merchant who visited Denmark in the tenth century later recalled: "Never before have I heard uglier songs than those of the Vikings in Denmark. The growling sound coming from their throats reminds me of dogs howling, only more untamed." Of course, that merchant likely did not hear the finest Viking singers. As for the songs they sang, almost none have survived. One possible exception is called "I Dreamed a Dream." It may have originated during the Viking Age and passed on orally from one generation to the next until it was written down in fourteenth-century Denmark.

Quoted in Mogens Friis, "Vikings and Their Music," The Vikings. www.viking.no/e/life/music/e-musikk-mogens.html.

Fighting for the Ball

Almost nothing is known about the rules and moves of the Norse ballgame knattleikr. *Nevertheless, according to Yngve Skråmm, an expert on Viking culture, the following facts have been determined about the game:*

[The players] were divided into teams; the teams were usually two against two though more could take part; a hard ball was hit by a bat; the opponent who didn't have the ball caught and threw the ball with his hands; body contact was allowed in the fight for the ball where the strongest had the best chance to win; the game demanded so much time that it was played from morning to night; there was a captain on each team; there were penalties and a penalty box; the playing field was lined; one had to change clothes for the game; it was played on the ice or grass.

Yngve Skråmm, "Knattleikr," The Vikings. www.viking.no/e/life/sports/eball.htm.

a ball, and the opposing players tried to tackle the person who caught the ball.

Games with strict rules, along with well-ordered towns, community assemblies and laws, and the vast trade networks spanning the Viking lands, demonstrate that the Norse were much more than raiders and pirates. Enemies, particularly foreign ones, had good reason to fear the Vikings. But within Norse society, respect for the law, traditional authority, property rights, and fair play were the rule rather than the exception.

Chapter Six

Viking Religion and Myths

The Vikings went through two basic stages or periods of religious beliefs and lore, the first pagan, the second Christian. As a belief system, Christianity emphasizes set rules of ethical behavior ordained by a single, all-powerful deity and interpreted by a class of holy individuals (priests) who serve that deity. "In Scandinavia before Christianity, however, no one would have understood this,"[53] scholar Julian D. Richards points out. The Norse pagan faith was more of a way of viewing the world and allowing humans to find workable ways of surviving in it. Instead of one perfect god, there were many imperfect gods who, like humans, had to fight to survive in a universe filled with chaos and uncertainty. "There was no strict religious discipline" in the Viking pagan faith, Wilson explains. "There was no recognized doctrine [set of beliefs and rules], no uniform method of worship. A man chose his own god and went his own way, calling on different gods in different circumstances."[54]

The Norse View of the World

The unique world pictured by the pre-Christian Vikings, a universe populated by a large number of gods and other superhuman beings and monsters, was described in a large collection of myths. Unfortunately, many of the original writings that recorded these tales are gone. Most of what is known today about Norse mythology comes from a handful of surviving sources. The most important is the *Prose Edda*, a retelling of the principal myths composed by Snorri Sturluson in the 1220s.

According to these tales, at the center of the universe lay a gigantic ash tree called Yggdrasil. "Its branches reached the sky and spread over the earth," wrote the late Magnus Magnusson, a

An illustration of a mounted warrior graces a fourteenth-century copy of Snorri Sturleson's Prose Edda.

The chief resident of Asgard was Odin, the leader of the main race of Norse gods, the Aesir. The oldest of their number, he possessed numerous powers and roles, including storm maker, war god, and master magician. Odin managed to maintain his high position in part because of these powers, but also because he could change his shape at will, which gave him a huge advantage over most opponents. Odin also had great wisdom. For that reason, Vikings of all walks of life lived by and enjoyed quoting his practical advice, which was handed down from one generation to another. Typical was a gem of Odinic wisdom from the ninth- or tenth-century document the *Havamal*, or "Sayings of the High One": "Only a fool lies awake all night and broods over his problems. When morning comes, he is worn out and his troubles [are] the same as before."[56] According to Viking mythology, Odin ruled over an estate in Asgard called Valhalla, the "Hall of the Heroes," where the souls of Viking warriors went. When a hero fell in battle, several angel-like female warriors—the Valkyries—guided him to Valhalla.

According to the *Prose Edda*, there were a number of other mighty gods. Among them was Odin's son Thor, a warrior deity who could command the elements, including wind, thunder, and lightning. Wolf describes him as

the defender of the Aesir against their natural enemies, the giants and giantesses. His weapon was the

leading authority on the Vikings. "At its base lay the Spring or Well of Fate, the source of all wisdom, tended by the three Norns [equivalent to the Greco-Roman Fates] who decided the destiny of all living creatures."[55] The great tree's three major roots led to three realms. The lowest was Niflheim, the world of the dead. Further up was Midgard, where humans lived, and above that loomed Asgard, the realm of the gods, connected to Midgard by a rainbow bridge called Bifrost.

hammer, Mjollnir, with which he held the forces of chaos in check. He also possessed a pair of iron gloves with which to grasp the hammer and a belt. And when he girded himself with the belt, his divine strength was doubled.[57]

Other important Norse gods included Odin's wife Frigg; Thor's wife Sif; Ty, god of justice; Freyja, goddess of love; Loki, the "trickster," who was part god and part demon; and Loki's daughter Hel, who oversaw the ghastly realm of the dead. (The familiar phrase "go to

The deities Odin, Thor, and Frey are depicted in stately poses on a Norse tapestry made in Sweden in the twelfth century.

Red-Headed Thor
and His Hammer

A noted scholar of the Norse, H.R.E. Davidson, here describes Odin's famous son, Thor:

I n the myths, Thor appears as a burly, red-headed man, immensely strong, with a huge appetite, blazing eyes, and a beard, full of enormous vitality and power. He could increase his strength by wearing a special belt of might. Other prize possessions of his were his great gloves, enabling him to grasp and shatter rocks, the chariot drawn by goats which took him across the sky, and his hammer. This last was regarded as the greatest of all the treasures of Asgard [the heavenly home of the Norse gods], for

Thor and his hammer formed a protection against the giants and the monsters, the enemies of gods and men.

H.R.E. Davidson, *Scandinavian Mythology.* New York: Peter Bedrick, 1986, pp. 59–60.

Unlike the chariots of ancient Greek gods, which were drawn by horses, Thor's chariot was pulled by goats, as captured in this dynamic early modern wood-cut.

hell" derives from "go to Hel," meaning to die in Old Norse.)

One unique attribute of the Norse gods was that the ultimate future both they and their human counterparts faced was terribly hopeless and bleak. Eventually, the Norse myths foretold, there would ensue an enormous battle called Ragnarok, or the "Twilight of the Gods." In this bloody fight, the Aesir and their allies, the humans, would square off against the forces of evil, and the evil ones would win. Both the gods and humanity would be destroyed. Yet in spite of knowing about this grim reality in advance, the gods and humans would refuse to surrender and instead fight on to the bitter end.

Norse Religious Rituals

As for how the Vikings worshiped the gods whose gloomy future they shared, not much is known. Following the conversion of the Norse lands to Christianity, church officials purposely suppressed and eventually destroyed most of the existing writings that described Scandinavian pagan rituals and/or contained pagan prayers. Over the centuries, therefore, these and many other elements of the older faith were lost and forgotten. But thanks to the tireless work of archaeologists, modern experts have been able to put together an approximate picture of pagan Viking worship.

First, rituals took place mostly in private settings. For instance, a few worshipers congregating in a barn on a farm belonging to one of them would have been quite common. Also, some special holy places, called *ve*, were located in the countryside, mainly in forests. There, people carved wooden figures of gods and prayed to them.

They also took part in the ritual of sacrifice (*blota*, which was also the word for worship in general). This involved the slaughter of goats, cattle, and other animals, whose blood and hides were thought to please the gods. Sometimes a worshiper placed the head, or even the whole carcass, of a dead beast above the door of his or her house. This act was intended as a way of giving thanks to one or more gods for some beneficial aid, for example an abundant harvest or success in a raid or battle. Such good fortune, the Norse believed, might also result from the worshiper's wearing or carrying an amulet, an object that people thought held various magical properties. Viking amulets were often composed of wood or metal and shaped like gods or the weapons or symbols of those deities.

Archaeologists have found both amulets and the remains of sacrificed animals in excavated Norse gravesites. Some pagan Vikings placed not only animals, but also food, weapons, and other goods in their graves because they believed in an afterlife. It was thought that the deceased person would require these items in the world beyond. However, not all Vikings accepted the notion of the afterlife. According to a number of surviving accounts, an unknown percentage of the population thought that one's earthly life was all there was and that

These stone grave markers were set in place more than nine centuries ago in a Danish Viking burial ground

no soul or other spark of that life survived death.

Whatever their beliefs about life after death, all Vikings followed certain rituals when someone died. The custom was for family members or close friends to prepare the body for cremation or burial. As one modern expert puts it:

The first act was usually to close the nostrils, mouth, and eyes. Often, the body was washed and the head wrapped in a cloth. If the death occurred at home, the body was sometimes carried away by a special route to the place of burial. The latter was a precaution taken if it was feared that the dead person would become an evil dead walker [zombie], who might return and harm the living. Although the dead were generally regarded as guardians watching [out for] the family . . . persons who had disgraced themselves in death became outcast ancestors and would typically roam as ghosts.[58]

Fending Off the Inevitable

That some Norse did not believe in an afterlife, and those that did thought people might return as perverse monsters, in a way mirrored the pessimistic view that all pagan Vikings had about the bleak future of both their race and their gods. These negative and discouraging

Helpless Before Evil

The Norse viewed Ragnarok, the "Twilight of the Gods," as the final battle between the deities and their enemies, a fight the gods would lose. About this seemingly hopeless view of the future, the late, renowned mythologist Edith Hamilton wrote:

Asgard, the home of the gods, is unlike any other heaven men have dreamed of. No radiancy of joy is in it, no assurance of bliss. It is a grave and solemn place, over which hangs the threat of an inevitable doom. The gods know that a day will come when they will be destroyed. . . . Asgard will fall in ruins. The cause the forces of good are fighting to defend against the forces of evil is hopeless. Nevertheless, the gods will fight for it to the end. Necessarily, the same is true of humanity. If the gods are finally helpless before evil, men and women must be more so. . . . In the last battle between good and evil, they will fight on the side of the gods and die with them.

Edith Hamilton, *Mythology*. New York: Grand Central, 1999, p. 300.

religious views may have developed to some degree due to the realities of life in ancient and early medieval Scandinavia. The inhabitants of that region, as well as Iceland and several other lands the Vikings colonized, experienced long, cold, harsh winters. The growing seasons of their crops were fairly brief, so food was often scarce. Also, the farms and villages where the vast majority of Norse lived were frequently separated by many miles, which forced them to deal with much more isolation and loneliness than most people experience today.

In the resulting relentless struggle for existence, it was perhaps only natural for the Vikings to develop a certain amount of negativism about life and the world. In the words of scholar H.R.E. Davidson, "Their experience of a savage world in which kingdoms were constantly set up and destroyed, with a background of stormy seas and long cold winter nights, gave a somber tinge to their picture of the realm of the gods."[59]

And yet, in stark contrast, these grim realties at the same time bred an attitude of defiance among many Norse, a sort of gallant refusal to allow fate's forbidding hand to hold them completely in its grip. This bold, tough approach to life appears often in the Vikings' stories about their cherished gods and heroes. Indeed, says Davidson, it "imparted a sturdy vigor to the figures who people their myths,"[60] in which strong, fearless characters repeatedly refuse to give in to fate. This is wonderfully illustrated by the fact that the Norse gods and their faithful human followers decided to try to win the battle of Ragnarok even though they knew in advance that they would lose.

Such attempts to fend off the inevitable can also be seen in the famous Norse myth of Loki's three monstrous children. They included the huge and terrifying serpent Jörmungandr, the fearsome goddess Hel, and the ferocious giant wolf Fenrir. The Norns, who could see far into the future, had predicted that when Ragnarok came, these three monsters would attack Asgard and the human world and bring about untold death and destruction. Odin and Thor seriously considered this prophecy and decided to try to alter that ordained destiny and bring about a more positive future.

To this end Odin gathered an army of valiant warriors, who managed to capture Loki's awful offspring—Jörmungandr, Hel, and Fenrir. Odin fearlessly grabbed hold of Jörmungandr, the hideous serpent, and tossed it into the deep sea that encircled Midgard. Odin hoped the serpent would drown. Instead, it sank to the bottom and over time grew even bigger than before. Next, Odin seized Hel, who was horribly ugly and smelled like rotten flesh. He threw her down into the depths of Niflheim, the land of the dead. Rather than losing her evil powers, however, she took charge of that dark realm and reshaped it to her own liking.

Finally, Odin approached the vicious and frightening Fenrir. The leader of the gods decided it would be best to confine the great wolf in Asgard, where he could keep a close watch on it. He ordered his

An Icelandic pen and ink drawing from the 1700s depicts the dramatic moment in a popular myth when Tyr loses his hand to the vicious wolf Fenrir.

"Heaven Is Rent in Twain"

This excerpt from Snorri Sturluson's description of Ragnarok in the Prose Edda *captures some of the high drama of the predicted final struggle between the forces of good and evil.*

The straight-standing ash [tree] Yggdrasil quivers, the old tree groans, and the [evil] giant gets loose. . . . Mountains dash together, giant maids are frightened, heroes go the way to Hel, and heaven is rent in twain. . . . All men abandon their homesteads when the warder of Midgard in wrath slays the serpent. The sun grows dark, the earth sinks into the sea, the bright stars from heaven vanish; fire rages, heat blazes, and high flames play against heaven itself.

Snorri Sturluson, *Prose Edda*, trans. Rasmus B. Anderson, Nothvegr Foundation. www.northvegr.org/lore/prose2/016.php.

blacksmiths to create a formidable iron chain and collar to bind Fenrir, but the monster quickly broke the chain. The blacksmiths forged other chains, but the beast merely laughed and shattered them all. Odin eventually acquired a magic chain fashioned by creatures called dark elves and with it was able to successfully restrain the giant wolf. However, Fenrir realized that time was on his side. If he waited patiently, he realized, the day of Ragnarok would eventually come and somehow he would find a way to get loose and unleash his vengeance on the gods and humans.

Thus, as the Norns had warned, no matter what Odin and the other gods did to try to stop the inevitable from happening, it would happen anyway. Yet even knowing this, Odin, and many Vikings in the real world, too, refused to give up.

They insisted on living as if the future would be bright rather than hopeless.

The Coming of Christianity

It was in large part because the Christian worldview offered a much more positive and hopeful future for both individuals and humanity as a whole that the Vikings began to convert to that faith. The idea that believers would be rewarded with eternal life in a peaceful heaven became increasingly appealing. By the early 1100s a majority of the Norse were Christians.

More precisely, most were partial Christians. For a while, an undetermined number of Vikings embraced both the new faith and some of the old pagan beliefs and rituals. Evidence for this syncretism (melding) of the two faiths appears partly in medallions and

The coming of Christianity to the Viking lands is commemorated by Gosforth Cross, in Cumberland, Britain. The cross features several carved scenes from Norse mythology.

other jewelry excavated from Viking gravesites. It was common, for example, to associate the Christian cross with Thor's famous hammer, Mjollnir, and to portray them side by side. In addition, archaeologists found a Norse cross with a Christian crucifixion scene carved on one side and a scene from Ragnarok on the other.

In time, however, the old beliefs faded and largely disappeared. More and more Christian churches came to dot the landscapes of Denmark, Norway, Iceland, and other Viking lands. The first Viking churches were small wooden structures that looked like houses. But by the early 1200s very large, multi-storied churches began to be erected.

"In Denmark and Sweden, wooden churches were replaced with stone from the 11th century onwards," Haywood writes,

> but in Norway the tradition of building with wood survived, and the 12th century saw remarkable developments in the architecture of the stave church [post-and-beam constructions with timber framing]. . . . Stave churches were tall, often elaborately decorated structures with carved portals [entrances], verandas, spires, and dragon-headed finials [sculptured ornaments], that have an almost oriental look about them. They must rank as some of the most distinctive monuments of the late Viking Age.[61]

In adopting Christianity, the Norse performed a complete reversal of attitude. Christian churches had once been nothing more to them than convenient, lucrative targets to be ransacked and looted. But eventually, the descendants of those raiders came to build their own churches and in that way became part of a great historical wheel coming full circle, with the invaders taking their places in the churches they had once destroyed.

Chapter Seven

Viking Explorations in the West

I n addition to their exploits as raiders, traders, and settlers, the Vikings were accomplished explorers. Nowhere else was this aspect of their achievements more noteworthy than in the region lying west of Scandinavia and northwest of the British Isles. This was, they found, an enormous area, encompassing several small island groups, Iceland, Greenland, and the seas surrounding them. But fortunately for them it contained islands, both large and small, spaced in such a way that settling on one island created a base from which to explore the one or ones lying farther west. As a result, in the space of about a century and a half, groups of Vikings island-hopped across the entire North Atlantic region. Eventually they reached the shores of North America, a full five centuries before Columbus did.

Some modern observers suggest that this series of discoveries and settlements was, given the Vikings' boldness

as a people and mastery of seafaring, almost unavoidable. According to Magnus Magnusson:

> There is an unbroken chain of inevitable progression between the discovery and subsequent settlement of, first, Iceland, then Greenland, and then Vinland [in North America]. The discovery and attempted settlement of Vinland were the logical outcomes of the great Scandinavian migrations that spilled over northern Europe in the early Middle Ages, the ultimate reach of the Norse surge to the west. It was on the Atlantic seaboard of North America that this huge impetus was finally exhausted.[62]

From Scotland to Greenland

The first stages of this seemingly relentless westward migration occurred in the ninth century soon after various

It was in this magnificent natural setting at Thingvelir, Iceland, that the island's national assembly, the Althing, periodically met.

Viking bands began settling parts of England and Scotland. Some of the Norse settlers sailed to the Shetland Islands, lying not far off Scotland's northern coast. And by the late 800s the Shetlands came under the direct rule of the Norwegian king.

The next step in the migration consisted of the 190-mile (306-km) hop to the windswept, mountainous Faeroe Islands, situated about 400 miles (644km) directly west of Norway. The first Vikings who landed there found that the islands were not completely uninhabited, as proved by a surviving description penned by an Irish monk in 825: "Some of these islands are very small. Nearly all are separated from the other by narrow sounds. On these islands hermits, who have sailed from [Ireland], have lived for roughly a hundred years."[63] The soil in the Faeroes was not suitable for large-scale farming. But the land easily supported the raising of sheep and cattle, which became the basis of the local Norse economy there.

Iceland lies about 200 miles (322km) northwest of the Faeroes, about the same distance as Britain lies south of

Visible are some of the remains of the Viking village at Hvalsey, in southern Greenland, one of the last and westernmost Viking settlements ever constructed.

them. So it is hardly surprising that enterprising Norse sailors soon discovered and explored the coasts of Iceland. Full-scale settlement of that highly volcanic island began around 870, and by 930 nearly all the good grazing lands along the coasts had been claimed. During that time, a form of national government was established. As in other Viking lands, local freemen in Iceland gathered at the local assemblies, or *things*, held in settlements spread across the island. They also formed the Althing, an assembly in which only chieftains could vote. The Althing settled disputes among the smaller assemblies and the villages they served. In time, the Althing began deciding island-wide policies. In about 1000, for example, its members agreed that Iceland should try to adopt Christianity. By that time, the island's population was well over thirty thousand.

Next came the exploration of Greenland, lying only a few hundred miles west of Iceland. Viking seafarers first sighted the larger island sometime in the early 900s. Initially they thought it was too cold and icebound to support settlements. But between 980 and 983 an expedition commanded by Erik the Red, who had been born in Norway and later settled in Iceland, located an ice-free region in the southwest. He managed to set up two main colonies. The first became known as the "Eastern" settlement. The other was the "Western" settlement, lying some 300 miles (483km) farther up the western coast.

These colonies, which soon came to support a total population of roughly three thousand, had a mixed economy. At the time, Greenland was in the midst of a warm period that featured much milder temperatures than exist there today. So some crops, including grains, could be grown. In addition, the inhabitants raised cattle and sheep, hunted walruses and polar bears, and traded with roving bands of the native inhabitants—the Eskimo, or Inuit.

Leif's Expedition

Once the Vikings were firmly planted in western Greenland, the stage was set, so to speak, for the discovery of North America, parts of which were situated only a few hundred miles due west. That fateful discovery took place around the year 986. On his way to the Greenland colonies from Norway, Bjarni Herjolfsson, a Viking merchant, was blown off course. One of the most famous Icelandic documents, the *Greenlanders' Saga*, states that Bjarni first landed in Iceland but found that his father had left for Greenland. "I want to sail my ship to Greenland," Bjarni told his crew, "if you are willing to come with me." Apparently they *were* willing, for they

> put to sea as soon as they were ready and sailed for three days until land was lost to sight below the horizon. Then the fair wind failed and northerly winds and fog set in, and for many days they had no idea what their course was. After that they saw the sun again and were able to get their bearings. They hoisted sail and after a day's sailing

they sighted land. They discussed amongst themselves what country this might be. . . . They could see that the country was not mountainous, but was well-wooded and with low hills. So they put to sea again.[64]

Soon afterward, Bjarni and his crew found two more mysterious lands. One was flat and forested, the other "high and mountainous and topped by a glacier." Bjarni is said to have remarked, "This country seems to me to be worthless."[65] For that reason, he decided not to land. Instead, he pointed his vessel eastward and after a few days reached his original destination, Greenland.

Although Bjarni had not been impressed by the unknown lands he had sighted, other men in the Greenland colonies were excited about his discoveries and wanted to follow up on them. One of these daring individuals was Leif Eriksson, Erik the Red's son. Leif convinced Bjarni to join forces with him in a new expedition.

Navigating the North Atlantic

Noted American historian Samuel E. Morison penned these words about the efforts of Norse sailors to navigate in the wide and wild North Atlantic wilderness.

How could one cross the Atlantic and return with no compass? The Norsemen managed it by what through the ages has been called "latitude sailing." Once having found the Faeroes [islands], Iceland, and Cape Farwell of [southern] Greenland, the Norse navigators took the latitude of each place by crudely measuring the angular height of the North star—and you can do that with a notched stick. So, in preparing for an Atlantic voyage, they sailed along the coast of Norway until they reached the presumed latitude of their destination, then shoved off and sailed with the North Star square on their starboard beam by night. . . . In thick [cloudy] weather they had to steer "by guess and by God." When the weather cleared, their crude instrument called the "sun shadow-board" was broken out. This was a wooden disk on which concentric circles were marked.

. . . Floated in a bowl of water to make it level, this shadow-board at high noon would give a rough latitude, indicating how far the ship was off-course, and enable her to get on again.

Samuel E. Morison, *The European Discovery of America: The Northern Voyages, A.D. 500–1600.* New York: Oxford University Press, 1993, p. 34.

This authentic modern replica of Leif Erikson's ship, the Icelander, *is on display to the public in Keflavik, Iceland.*

The voyagers made it to at least three locations in northeastern North America. The first—the mountainous place with the glacier that Bjarni had seen on his earlier trip—they named Helluland, or "Flat Stone Land." The consensus of modern experts is that it was Canada's Baffin Island. Next, they reached a heavily forested region that Leif named Markland, meaning "Woodland." This was probably Labrador, also in what is now eastern Canada.

Two days after departing Markland, the explorers came to a country where it seemed that the winters were mild and the rivers filled with salmon. "They decided to winter there and built some large houses," the *Greenlanders'*

Saga says. They called the tiny village Leifsbudir, or "Leif's Camp." The same document claims that a few days later, while exploring the area, one of the men, named Tyrkir, made a crucial discovery. "I have some news," Tyrkir said. "I found vines and grapes." Leif asked, "Is that true?" And Tyrkir told him, "Of course it is true. Where I was born there were plenty of vines and grapes."[66] According to the story, the finding of the grape vines inspired Leif to call the place Vinland.

Where Was Vinland?

In later ages, particularly in the twentieth century, the exact location of Vinland became hotly debated. The first

Among the possible locations of Vinland are Cape Cod, in Massachusetts, and Narragansset Bay, in Rhode Island, both shown in this map of southern New England.

question that scholars wanted to answer was where Leif had erected his camp, Leifsbudir. The answer seemed to come in 1960, when Norwegian explorer Helge Ingstad and his archaeologist wife, Anne, uncovered the remains of a medieval Norse settlement at L'Anse aux Meadows, in northern Newfoundland. As explained by American historian Samuel E. Morison, among numerous other Viking artifacts the Ingstads found two great houses closely correspon-ding to the Norse dwellings earlier uncovered in Greenland. The big-ger is 70 feet long and 55 feet wide. The floors were of hard-pressed clay, the walls of turf, and the roof of timber, covered with sod. There is a central hall with a fire-pit in the center, and a little ember-box of flat stones in which coals were kept alive during the night. Around the fireplace are raised-earth benches which the Norsemen doubtless cov-ered with polar bear and other skins. One can imagine Leif and his [followers] lounging there at night

and exchanging tales about their former adventures.[67]

The Ingstads were able to date the site to about the year 1000, exactly when the sagas said that Leif's expedi-tion occurred. So they and other schol-ars became convinced that L'Anse aux Meadows was Leifsbudir. However, many were not so sure that Leif's set-tlement was also Vinland. "Here is the stumbling block," Morison says. "Wild grapes cannot possibly have grown as far north as L'Anse aux Meadows. Their utmost coastal limit in historic times has been southern Nova Scotia,

The Earth Is Round?

Some evidence suggests that at some point the Vikings realized the Earth is a sphere, though their explanations for that fact were often convoluted and flawed. In the following excerpt from a thirteenth-century Norwegian document, a father gives one of these explanations to his son.

If you take a lighted candle and set it in a room, you may expect it to light up the en-tire interior, unless something should hinder, though the room be quite large. But if you take an apple and hang it close to the flame, so near that it is heated, the apple will darken nearly half the room or even more. However, if you hang the apple near the wall, it will not get hot; the candle will light up the whole house; and the shadow on the wall where the apple hangs will be scarcely half as large as the apple itself. From this you may infer that the earth-circle is round like a ball and not equally near the sun at every point. But where the curved surface lies nearest the sun's path, there will the greatest heat be.

Laurence M. Larson, trans., *The King's Mirror*. www.mediumaevum.com/75years/mirror/sec1.html#V.

and they are not really abundant until you reach southern New England."[68]

It appears, therefore, that the building of Leifsbudir and the finding of the grapes occurred in two separate places, and the author of the saga later mistakenly assumed they were the same place. Most archaeologists now agree with Richard Hall, who suggests that Leif's village may well have been "an explorers' and exploiters' base, a way-station from which to range out in search of valuable natural resources that could be brought back [to the main camp] for storage."[69] If that is true, Vinland was probably located farther south, maybe in Maine, Cape Cod (in Massachusetts), or Narragansett Bay (in Rhode Island).

Voyages Long Forgotten

Wherever Vinland really was, scholars are more certain that Leif's expedition was not the last Norse venture to North America. The Icelandic sagas claim that three or four more voyages to that region took place between 1000 and 1030. Leif's brother Thorvald was in charge of one of these voyages. He had the second Viking encounter with Native Americans (the first being between the Greenlanders and Eskimo). Thorvald and his followers called them "Skraelings," meaning "wretches." "They were small and evil-looking," Thorvald claimed, "and their hair was coarse. They had large eyes and broad cheekbones."[70] For reasons that remain unclear, Thorvald and his men attacked the first natives they saw, and that led to at least two bloody battles. In the last one Thorvald himself was badly wounded and soon afterward died.

Thorfinn Karlsefni, a Viking mariner who lived in Iceland, led the next voyage to North America. Hoping to plant a permanent colony, he brought along more than sixty men, five women, and a large number of sheep and other animals. Thorfinn found Leifsbudir, and he and the others wintered there. During their stay, his pregnant wife had a child, a boy named Snorri, who had the distinction of being the first known person of European stock born in the Americas.

Thorfinn had no less trouble with the natives than Thorvald had. At first the two peoples traded peacefully with each other, but it was not long before they came to blows. Several people were killed on both sides. Probably the continuing danger these natives posed was the primary reason that in the spring, Thorfinn made the decision to abandon the mission and return to Greenland.

Poor relations with the Native Americans was not the only reason that the Vikings eventually gave up on colonizing North America. Evidence shows that the climates of both Newfoundland and Greenland were rapidly growing colder. Also, the Greenlanders came to realize that most of the natural resources they had found in North America could be imported more cheaply from Norway.

In addition, living in Greenland was a difficult struggle in and of itself. The small habitable sections of that island lacked the resources, both natural and human, to maintain, in addition to itself, a large colony lying hundreds of

A modern painting depicts one of the battles between Vikings and American Indians mentioned in the Norse sagas. The Vikings called the Indians "Skraelings."

miles away. And sure enough, in time the Vikings largely vacated Greenland, too. The last recorded contact between Iceland and the Greenland settlements was in 1410, and those few Viking farmers who stubbornly refused to leave the larger island died not long after that.

By that time the vast majority of Europeans had completely forgotten that those faraway Scandinavian colonies had ever existed. And when a Portuguese explorer, Gaspar Corte-Real, reached Greenland in 1500, he thought he was the first European person to see it. It was he who named it "Terra Verde" (Portuguese for Greenland). Gaspar and his crew certainly had no inkling of the once great era of Viking westward exploration. As scholar Irwin Unger puts it, "As far as Europe was concerned, it was as if the Norse discoveries had never been made."[71]

The End of the Viking Age

The vast majority of modern historians estimate the year 1066 as the end of the Viking Age. They realize, of course, that the Vikings did not suddenly disappear from the historical scene in a single year. Rather, that date is cited because it marked the last large-scale Norse military foray, led by the last great Viking warrior-adventurer —Norway's Harald (also Sigurdsson) Hardrada. As it turned out, 1066 became more famous as the year in which the Normans, under William the Conqueror, invaded England and won the Battle of Hastings. This was no coincidence, as the two events were closely related. The Normans, hailing from northwestern France, were themselves former Vikings, whose recent absorption into European society was another pivotal marker of the waning of the Viking era.

Assimilation and Conversion

Indeed, the assimilation (the process of one cultural group being absorbed into another) of large numbers of traditional Viking warriors into the very kingdoms and peoples they had once attacked and looted was the principal reason for the eventual disappearance of old-style Norse culture. And the rise of the Normans was a prime example.

In the late 800s increasing resistance by local Frankish leaders and armies largely foiled the efforts of the Vikings who had been attacking France. In 892 these Vikings turned their attention to raiding Britain and began using northwestern France as a base for those attacks. In 911 their leader, Rollo, made a deal with the Frankish monarch Charles the Simple. Rollo agreed to give Charles his allegiance and to convert to Christianity, and in return Rollo became a Frankish noble with control over large tracts of land and thousands of Frankish peasants.

Charles's main intention was to make these converted Norse a buffer that would blunt any further Viking raids on France. And this worked. The Vikings in northwestern France permanently settled down, and although that region became known thereafter as Normandy, or "Northman's land," they rapidly blended with the local Franks. Within two generations Normandy's residents of Scandinavian stock thought of themselves as Franks, not as Vikings.

The same process was underway in other parts of Europe and beyond. In Russia in the 900s, for example, Viking settlers steadily absorbed local Slavic names and culture. And by 1050 or so, as Haywood says, "the Rus were thoroughly Slavic in character."[72]

In Russia, as in France and other areas, a key part of the process of assimilation was conversion to Christianity. On the one hand, abandoning their pagan beliefs and rituals in favor of Christian ones made the converted Vikings culturally more like their former enemies. On the other hand, switching to Christianity made it easier for Norse leaders to control their subjects. This was because they could now claim that their rule was divinely inspired and ordained by God. Also, as Christians, these rulers could more easily make deals with existing European Christian kingdoms. In these ways, the Scandinavian upper classes gained new ways of acquiring wealth and prestige. Raiding and other old-style Viking ways were no longer necessary.

Their Physical and Cultural DNA

While these religious and cultural conversions were occurring throughout Europe, a handful of Viking leaders tried to maintain their traditional Norse identities and ways. The most famous and in many ways most colorful example was the last great Viking, Harald Sigurdsson. Over time, his violent, cold-blooded, old-style Viking tactics earned him the nickname of Hardrada, meaning "ruthless." The half brother of a former Norwegian king, as a young man he became involved in civil strife in Norway and eventually fled to Russia. There he worked as a mercenary soldier for various local Rus princes and also served for a few years as one of the prestigious Varangian Guards in Constantinople.

In 1045 Harald returned to Norway and became joint ruler with King Magnus. Two years later Magnus died, leaving Harald sole ruler.

After many years of fruitless attempts to defeat the king of Denmark for mastery of Scandinavia, in 1066 Harald decided to invade England and amassed between 240 and 300 ships and more than 10,000 soldiers for that purpose. He won a major victory that year at Fulford, near York.

But five days later he was disastrously defeated and killed (by an arrow to the throat) at nearby Stamford Bridge by England's King Harold Godwinsson. *The Anglo-Saxon Chronicle* recorded:

Harald Sigurdsson, last of the great Viking rulers, is killed in the battle of Stamford Bridge, in 1066.

Thither came Harold, king of the English . . . against them beyond the bridge; and they closed together there, and continued long in the day fighting very severely. There was slain Harald [the] king of Norway [and] a multitude of people . . . both [Northmen] and English. . . . Some [Northmen] were drowned, some burned to death, and thus variously destroyed; so that there was little left, and the English gained possession of the field.[73]

Harold's stunning victory turned out to be a hollow one, however. Hearing that William of Normandy was landing troops in southern England, he raced his exhausted men southward. Nineteen days later, Harold lay dead on the field of Hastings. The irony was that, after crushing the last great Viking army near York, the English king was himself overcome by soldiers whose great grandfathers had been Vikings.

And the victors of Hastings subsequently contributed their physical and cultural DNA to the steadily rising English nation. In this and similar ways, the Viking heritage melded with and became inseparable from the greater heritage of Europe itself.

Notes

Introduction: Surviving Evidence for the Vikings

1. David M. Wilson, *The Vikings and Their Origins*. London: Thames and Hudson, 2001, p. 65.
2. Quoted in James H. Todd, trans., *Wars of the Gaedhil with the Gaill*. London: Longmans, Green, 1867, pp. 51–52.
3. James Ingram, trans., *The Anglo-Saxon Chronicle*, Online Medieval and Classical Library. http://omacl.org/Anglo/part.html.
4. Ingram, *The Anglo-Saxon Chronicle*.
5. Quoted in James E. Montgomery, "Ibn Fadlan and the Rusiyyah," Cornell University Library. www.library.cornell.edu/colldev/mideast/montgol.pdf.
6. Richard Hall, *The World of the Vikings*. London: Thames and Hudson, 2007, p. 8.
7. Snorri Sturlusun, The Chronicle of the Kings of Norway, Project Gutenberg. www.gutenberg.orgfiles/598/598-h/598-h.htm#2H_PREF.
8. Brenda R. Lewis, "Jorvik: the Viking City of York," TimeTravel-Britain.com.www.timetravelbritain.com/articles/towns/jorvik.shtml.
9. Hall, *The World of the Vikings*, p. 11.

Chapter One: Viking Origins and Early Raids

10. Quoted in Howard La Fay, *The Vikings*. Washington, DC: National Geographic, 1972, p. 74.
11. Quoted in Henry Loyn, *The Vikings in Britain*. Hoboken, NJ: Wiley-Blackwell, 1995, pp. 55-56.
12. John Haywood, *The Penguin Historical Atlas of the Vikings*. New York: Penguin, 1995, pp. 8-9.
13. Pliny the Elder, *Natural History*, excerpted in *Pliny the Elder: Natural History: A Selection*, trans. John H. Healy. New York: Penguin, 1991, p. 34.
14. Tacitus, *Germania*, in *Tacitus: The Agricola and Germania*, trans. Harold Mattingly. New York: Penguin, 1986, p. 138.
15. Wilson, *The Vikings and Their Origins*, p. 11.
16. Wilson, *The Vikings and Their Origins*, p. 65.
17. Saxo Grammaticus, *History of the Danes*, Northvegr Foundation. www.northvegr.org/lore/saxo/000_14.php.
18. Haywood, *The Penguin Historical Atlas of the Vikings*, p. 20.
19. Hall, *The World of the Vikings*, p. 67.
20. Hall, *The World of the Vikings*, p. 67.

Chapter Two: Viking Conquests and Expansion

21. Quoted in La Fay, *The Vikings*, p. 8.
22. Ingram, *Anglo-Saxon Chronicle*.
23. Ingram, *Anglo-Saxon Chronicle*.
24. Hall, *The World of the Vikings*, p. 95.

25. Quoted in James Graham-Campbell, *The Viking World*. New York: Ticknor and Fields, 2006, pp. 31-32.
26. Ingram, *Anglo-Saxon Chronicle.*
27. Ingram, *Anglo-Saxon Chronicle.*
28. Quoted in La Fay, *The Vikings*, p. 53.
29. Quoted in Rene Chartrand et al, *The Vikings: Voyagers of Discovery and Plunder*. Oxford, Eng.: Osprey, 2006, p. 56.
30. Wilson, *The Vikings and Their Origins*, p. 94.

Chapter Three: Viking Warriors and Ships

31. Snorri Sturluson, "Ynglinga Saga," *Heimskringla*, Online Medieval and Classical Library. http://omacl.org/Heimskringla/ynglinga.html.
32. Graham-Campbell, *The Viking World*, p. 24.
33. Ian Heath, *The Vikings*. Oxford: Osprey, 2001, pp. 50-51.
34. Snorri Sturluson, Heimskringla, Project Gutenberg. www.gutenberg.org/files/598/598-h/598-h.htm#2H_4_0204.
35. Heath, *The Vikings*, p. 32.
36. Snorri Sturluson, *Heimskringla.*
37. Haywood, *The Penguin Historical Atlas of the Vikings*, pp. 40–41.
38. Sturluson, *Heimskringla.*

Chapter Four: Viking Families and Home Life

39. Graham-Campbell, *The Viking World*, p. 10.
40. Kirsten Wolf, *Daily Life of the Vikings*. Westport, CT: Greenwood, 2004, p. 74.
41. Quoted in Amanda Graham, "The Voyage of Ohthere from King Alfred's Orosius," Yukon College, 2001.

http://ycdl4.yukoncollege.yk.ca/~agraham//nost202/ottar.htm.
42. Wolf, *Daily Life of the Vikings*, p. 8.
43. Ornolfur Thorsson, ed., *The Sagas of the Icelanders: A Selection*. New York: Viking, 2000, pp. 278-279.
44. Wolf, *Daily Life of the Vikings*, p. 13.
45. "The Song of Rig," from "The Elder Edda," Internet Archive. www.archive.org/stream/elderorpoeticedd01brayuoft/elderorpoeticedd01brayuoft_djvu.txt.
46. Quoted in Montgomery, "Ibn Fadlan and the Rusiyyah."
47. Quoted in Montgomery, "Ibn Fadlan and the Rusiyyah."

Chapter Five: Viking Communities and Culture

48. Graham-Campbell, *The Viking World*, pp. 93, 95.
49. Laurence M. Larson, trans., *The King's Mirror*. www.mediumaevum.com/75years/mirror/index.html.
50. Larson, *The King's Mirror.*
51. Quoted in La Fay, *The Vikings*, p. 19.
52. Wolf, *Daily Life of the Vikings*, p. 47.

Chapter Six: Viking Religion and Myths

53. Julian D. Richards, *The Vikings: A Very Short Introduction*. New York: Oxford University Press, 2005, p. 20.
54. Wilson, *The Vikings and Their Origins*, pp. 15-16.
55. Magnus Magnusson, *Hammer of the North: Myths and Heroes of the Viking Age*. New York: Putnam, 1986, p. 49.
56. Quoted in Chartrand et al, *The Vikings: Voyagers of Discovery and Plunder*, p. 40.
57. Wolf, *Daily Life of the Vikings*, p. 150.

58. Wolf, *Daily Life of the Vikings,* pp. 158-159.
59. H.R.E. Davidson, *Scandinavian Mythology.* New York: Peter Bedrick Books, 1986, p. 8.
60. Davidson, *Scandinavian Mythology,* p. 8.
61. Haywood, *The Penguin Historical Atlas of the Vikings,* pp. 132–133.

Chapter Seven: Viking Explorations in the West

62. Magnus Magnusson and Hermann Palsson, trans., *The Vinland Sagas.* New York: New York University Press, 1978, p. 11.
63. Quoted in La Fay, *The Vikings,* p. 118.
64. Quoted in Magnusson and Palsson, *The Vinland Sagas,* pp. 52–53.
65. Quoted in Magnusson and Palsson, *The Vinland Sagas,* p. 53.
66. Quoted in Magnusson and Palsson, *The Vinland Sagas,* pp. 56–57.
67. Samuel E. Morison, *The European Discovery of America: The Northern Voyages, A.D. 500–1600.* New York: Oxford University Press, 1993, p. 49.
68. Morison, *The European Discovery of America,* p. 51.
69. Hall, *The World of the Vikings,* p. 163.
70. Quoted in Magnusson and Palsson, *The Vinland Sagas,* p. 98.
71. Irwin Unger, *These United States: The Questions of Our Past.* Boston: Little, Brown, 2002, p. 5.

Epilogue: The End of the Viking Age

72. Haywood, *The Penguin Historical Atlas of the Vikings,* p. 108.
73. Ingram, *Anglo-Saxon Chronicle.* http://omacl.org/Anglo/part5.html.

Glossary

amulet: An object, either worn or carried, thought to have magical properties.

berserker: A legendary Viking warrior who fought with seemingly inhuman strength.

blota: Sacrifice, or religious offerings.

bóndi: Viking freemen.

byrnie: A mail shirt (see mail).

clinkering: A ship construction method in which the hull boards overlap.

cremation: Burning of the dead.

Danegold: A bribe paid to Viking warriors to keep them from attacking.

Danelaw: A large sector of eastern England taken over by the Vikings in early medieval times.

dowry: Money or valuables supplied by a bride's father for her upkeep in her marriage.

Glima: A form of Viking wrestling that resembled modern Judo.

Hnefatafl: A medieval board game similar to chess.

inhumation: Burial of the dead.

jarl: "Earl"; a member of the Norse noble or upper class.

keel: The central spine running lengthwise along the bottom of a ship's hull.

knattleikr: A Viking ballgame that may have featured elements of both baseball and football.

langskip: "Longship"; a Viking warship.

longphort: A fortified central military base.

mail (or chain mail): A kind of armor consisting of a shirt or jerkin made of pieces of metal or with the pieces attached.

Morels: A medieval board game similar to checkers.

pagan: Non-Christian.

rune: A letter or character in the medieval Germanic writing system known as runic.

Rus: Vikings who settled in what is now Russia.

saga: An epic story; the Icelandic sagas featured Viking heroes, gods, and other important figures.

shield-wall: A battlefield formation in which fighters stood close together with their shields touching or overlapping.

skald: A Viking storyteller-singer.

skei: A Viking warship with more than fifty-six oars.

snekkja: A Viking warship with forty to fifty-six oars.

strakes: Hull boards on a Viking ship.

thatch: Thickly interwoven tree branches, often used for roofing in medieval times.

thing: An assembly, or meeting, of Viking freemen.

thrall: A Viking slave.

threttnessa: A Viking warship with twenty-six oars.

tribute: Money or valuables paid to acknowledge one's submission to someone stronger.

ve: Holy sites in the countryside where Vikings performed religious rituals.

wattle-and-daub: A construction technique common in medieval Europe that featured interwoven branches coated with a paste made of clay or dung.

zoomorphic: An artistic style built around images of animals.

For More Information

Books

Rene Chartrand et al., *The Vikings: Voyagers of Discovery and Plunder*. Oxford: Osprey, 2006. A collection of long, detailed essays on Viking history and culture, accompanied by stunning artwork.

Eric Christiansen, *The Norsemen in the Viking Age*. Hoboken, NJ: Wiley-Blackwell, 2006. One of the best books about the Vikings, with much up-to-date information.

H.R.E. Davidson, *Gods and Myths of Northern Europe*. Baltimore: Penguin, 1984. One of the best general overviews of Norse mythology, written by one of the acknowledged experts in the field.

Keith Durham, *Viking Longship*. Oxford: Osprey, 2002. Provides much valuable information about how Viking ships were constructed and used.

Robert Ferguson, *The Vikings: A History*. New York: Viking, 2009. A fine synopsis of the Viking Age and those who peopled it.

James Graham-Campbell, *The Viking World*. New York: Ticknor and Fields, 2006. An excellent general overview of the Vikings and their civilization.

Richard Hall, *The World of the Vikings*. London: Thames and Hudson, 2007. One of the better recent studies of the Norse, including much data on archaeological finds relating to Viking culture. Also beautifully illustrated.

Mark Harrison, *Viking Hersir: 793–1066 A.D.* Oxford: Osprey, 1993. Contains a great deal of solid information about Norse weapons and warfare.

John Haywood, *The Penguin Historical Atlas of the Vikings*. New York: Penguin, 1995. A fine brief overview of Viking history, with numerous excellent maps and photos.

Ian Heath, *The Vikings*. Oxford: Osprey, 2001. A short but information-packed look at Viking history and weapons.

Tony Horwitz, *A Voyage Long and Strange: On the Trail of Vikings, Conquistadors, Lost Colonists and Other Adventurers in Early America*. New York: Macmillan, 2009. Discusses Norse explorations of North America.

Gwyn Jones, *A History of the Vikings*. New York: Oxford University Press, 2001. One of the better modern studies of Viking history, this is extremely well researched and highly detailed.

Magnus Magnusson, *Hammer of the North: Myths and Heroes of the Viking Age*. New York: Putnam, 1986. A very useful examination of the major Viking myths and heroes.

Magnus Magnusson and Hermann Palsson, trans., *The Vinland Sagas*. New York: New York University Press, 1978. An excellent translation of the *Greenlanders' Saga* and *Erik the Red's Saga*, key documents on the Viking voyages to North America.

Samuel E. Morison, *The European Discovery of America: The Northern Voyages, A.D. 500–1600*. New York: Oxford University Press, 1993. This award-winning book by a great historian contains a long chapter on the Norse transatlantic voyages.

Julian D. Richards, *The Vikings: A Very Short Introduction*. New York: Oxford University Press, 2005. Though short, this book contains many useful facts about the Vikings.

Ornolfur Thorsson, ed., *The Sagas of the Icelanders: A Selection*. New York: Viking, 2000. A large compilation containing English translations of many of the Icelandic sagas.

David M. Wilson, *The Vikings and Their Origins*. London: Thames and Hudson, 2001. A fairly brief but thoughtful and well-written look at Viking culture.

Kirsten Wolf, *Daily Life of the Vikings*. Westport, CT: Greenwood, 2004. One of the best general studies of everyday life among Scandinavians and other Norse during the Viking Age.

Web Sites

Explore a Viking Village (www.pbs.org/wgbh/nova/vikings/village.html). An excellent site provided by the Public Broadcasting Service (PBS) containing several videos, each of which takes the viewer on a journey through a separate part of a Viking village.

Secrets of Norse Ships (www.pbs.org/wgbh/nova/vikings/ships.html). An informative PBS *Nova* site about the construction and uses of Viking ships.

The Vikings (www.viking.no/e/index.html). This site has many links that lead to short, readable articles about different aspects of Viking life.

Vikings (www.crystalinks.com/vikings.html). A large site provided by Crystalinks, packed with information about the Vikings. Includes several helpful maps.

Vikings: The North Atlantic Saga (www.mnh.si.edu/vikings). A companion Web site for an exhibition about Viking explorations at the National Museum of Natural History.

Index

Picture Credits

Cover, © Stefano Bianchetti/Corbis
© Doug Steley/Alamy, 44
© Ilja Dubovskis/Alamy, 26
© Skyscan Photolibrary/Alamy, 18
Art Resource, NY, 55
Werner Forman/Art Resource, NY, 6 (upper), 50, 76, 77, 85, 88
HIP/Art Resource, NY, 11, 45
Erich Lessing/Art Resource, NY, 6 (lower), 23
National Trust Photo Library/Art Resource, NY, 42-43
Battle of Stamford Bridge, 1870 (oil on canvas) by Arbo, Peter Nicolai (1831-92) Private Collection/Photo
    O. Vaering/The Bridgeman Art Library, 99
The Funeral of a Viking, 1893 (oil on canvas) by Dicksee, Sir Frank (1853-1928)/Manchester Art Gallery,
    UK/The Bridgeman Art Library, 62
The Vikings; The Sea-Warriors by English School, (20th century) Private Collection/Look and
    Learn/The Bridgeman Art Library, 9
Edmund king of East Anglia killed by the Danes, Doyle, James E. (19th Century) Private
    Collection/Look and Learn/The Bridgeman Art Library, 35
Britain's First Naval Battle, illustration from "British Battles on Land and Sea," published by Cassell,
    London, c. 1910 (litho) by Forrestier, A. (fl. 1910) Private Collection/The Bridgeman Art Library, 51
Leif Ericsson's men being attacked by indians by Frey, Oliver (b. 1948) Private Collection/Look and
    Learn/The Bridgeman Art Library, 96
The Viking Sea Raiders by Goodwin, Albert (1845-1932) Private Collection/Christopher Wood Gallery,
    London, UK/The Bridgeman Art Library, 27
Vikings by Jackson, Peter (1922-2003) Private Collection /Look and Learn/The Bridgeman Art Library,
    39
The Norse god Tyr losing his hand to the bound wolf, Fenrir (pen & ink on paper) by Icelandic School,
    (18th century) Royal Library, Copenhagen, Denmark/The Bridgeman Art Library, 83
A Shire-Moot in Saxon times, illustration from "The History of the Nation" (litho) by English School,
    (20th century) Private Collection/The Stapleton Collection/The Bridgeman Art Library, 69
Model of the fortress at Trelleborg (mixed media) by Museet ved Trellegorg, Slagelse, Denmark/Ancient
    Art and Architecture Collection Ltd./The Bridgeman Art Library International, 30
© Bettman/Corbis, 78
© Russ Hein/All Canada Photos/Corbis, 56
© Rolf Hicker/All Canada Photos/Corbis, 7 (upper)
© Wolfgang Kaehler/Corbis, 15, 89
© Frank Lukasseck/Corbis, 92
© Ted Speigel/Corbis, 54, 65
© Homer Sykes/Corbis, 72
© Frank Zaska/Corbis, 59
Jeff J. Mitchell/Getty Images, 47
Rischgitz/Hulton Archive/Getty Images, 7 (lower)
Michael Hampshire/National Geographic/Getty Images, 66
Ted Speigel/National Geographic/Getty Images, 80
Paul Popper/Popperfoto/Getty Images, 71
© North Wind Picture Archives, 33, 93

About the Author

In addition to his acclaimed volumes on the ancient world, historian Don Nardo has produced several studies of medieval times, including *Life on a Medieval Pilgrimage*, *The Medieval Castle*, *The Italian Renaissance*, *The Inquisition*, and a biography of medieval astronomer Tycho Brahe. He has also produced volumes about medieval warfare, the King Arthur legends, and the age of exploration. Mr. Nardo, who in addition composes orchestral music, resides with his wife Christine in Massachusetts.